ABOUT THE AUTHOR

Hello, and welcome to an enriching culinary experience. I'm Bianca Sealey, a chef and culinary enthusiast who has embraced the world of nutrition, focusing on flavorful, health-conscious cooking. A deep-rooted family passion for food and wellness nurtured my journey into the culinary arts and nutritious eating.

Growing up, I was always surrounded by the aromas and flavors of dishes lovingly prepared in family kitchens, where recipes were more than just instructions, they were stories passed down through generations. This environment ignited my passion for cooking and the desire to explore the nutritional aspects of our foods.

Over the years, this interest blossomed into a broader exploration of dietary practices, immersing me in various food philosophies backed by extensive research, studies, and real-life experiences.
It's been a journey of discovery, learning how the art of cooking intersects with our overall health and well-being.

Creating this book has been a journey of love, combining my culinary skills with the knowledge I've gained about nutrition. This book isn't just a compilation of recipes; it's a testament to a lifelong passion for cooking, a guide for those eager to infuse their meals with taste and health, and a tribute to the culinary wisdom inherited from my family.

As a chef and a fellow food lover, I am excited to share the insights and delicious creations that have shaped my understanding of nutritious cooking. I aim to make healthy eating both enjoyable and approachable for everyone.

Thank you for choosing this book and allowing me to join your culinary adventure. Whether you're just starting to explore the art of healthy cooking or seeking to enrich your existing skills, I hope to provide you with the recipes, techniques, and inspiration you need to craft delightful, nourishing meals.

With Warm Regards,
Bianca Sealey

1

WHAT IS THE KETOGENIC DIET?

The ketogenic diet, a nutritional regimen defined by its low carbohydrate, moderate protein, and high fat intake, fundamentally reconfigures the body's energy processing. At its core lies the metabolic state of ketosis, a shift from relying on glucose, primarily derived from carbohydrates, to utilizing fats as the main energy source.

Ketosis, a natural metabolic response to the body's reduced carbohydrate intake, is initiated when carbohydrate consumption is reduced to about 20-50 grams daily. This reduction depletes the body's glucose reserves, prompting the liver to metabolize fats into ketone bodies. Once released into the bloodstream, these ketones become the primary energy substrate, supplanting glucose.

This metabolic transition is not merely about altering food intake; it represents a profound shift in how the body conserves and expends energy. Initially, the ketogenic diet's primary role was therapeutic, developed in the early 20th century as a treatment for epilepsy. However, its scope has expanded over time, with research uncovering benefits in weight management, metabolic health, and neurological function, particularly pertinent for those over 60.

The ketogenic diet's significance lies in its capacity for weight reduction and its impact on overall metabolic processes. By switching to a fat- and ketone-based energy system, the diet can lead to decreased blood sugar levels and improved insulin sensitivity. The consistent energy supply provided by ketones is also associated with enhanced mental clarity and sustained energy levels, benefits that are increasingly valuable as we age.

Distinct from other low-carb diets, the ketogenic approach is meticulously balanced in its macronutrient distribution. It emphasizes high fat intake—about 70-80% of daily calories—alongside moderate protein and minimal carbohydrates, a combination essential for maintaining the state of ketosis.

Distinct from other low-carb diets, the ketogenic approach is meticulously balanced in its macronutrient distribution. It emphasizes high fat intake—about 70-80% of daily calories—alongside moderate protein and minimal carbohydrates, a combination essential for maintaining the state of ketosis

ORIGINS AND HISTORY OF THE KETOGENIC DIET.

The ketogenic diet has a rich and varied history that dates back to the early 20th century. Its origin, deeply rooted in medical science, was primarily as a treatment for epilepsy.

Dr. Russell Wilder of the Mayo Clinic was pivotal in developing the ketogenic diet in 1921. His goal was to create a diet that mirrored the benefits of fasting, which had been observed to significantly reduce the frequency and severity of seizures in epileptic patients. This was a groundbreaking approach at the time, as fasting was effective but needed to be more sustainable as a long-term treatment strategy.

The diet quickly gained traction as a therapeutic tool for managing epilepsy, particularly in children who didn't respond well to available medications. The mechanism behind its effectiveness was intriguing: by drastically reducing carbohydrate intake and replacing it with fat, the body entered a state of ketosis, similar to that achieved through fasting, which had a notable impact on reducing seizures.

However, the diet's prominence in the field of epilepsy treatment began to decline with the introduction of new anticonvulsant drugs in the mid-20th century. These medications offered an easier and more conventional approach to seizure management, leading to a decrease in the use of the ketogenic diet in clinical settings.

It was in the late 20th century that the ketogenic diet re-emerged, this time gaining attention beyond its original therapeutic purpose. Researchers began exploring its potential benefits in other areas, such as weight management, metabolic health, and even neurological conditions beyond epilepsy. This resurgence was partly driven by cases where traditional medications for epilepsy were ineffective, highlighting the diet's continued relevance in this field.

In recent years, the diet has been embraced for its medical benefits and as a lifestyle choice for individuals seeking to improve their overall health and wellness. This expanded interest has led to further research and a better understanding of the diet's mechanisms and potential applications in various health contexts.

The ketogenic diet's journey from medical treatment to a popular lifestyle choice underscores its versatility and enduring relevance in nutrition and health. Its historical roots provide valuable insights into its mechanisms and potential, particularly for older adults seeking to optimize their health and well-being through dietary choices

BIOCHEMICAL PRINCIPLES: HOW THE BODY TRANSITIONS FROM GLYCOLYSIS TO KETOSIS.

The transition from glycolysis to ketosis is a key biochemical principle behind the ketogenic diet. It's a shift in how our bodies create energy, moving from a reliance on sugars to burning fats. Let's break this down to understand it better.

Normally, our bodies use a process called glycolysis to generate energy. When we eat foods containing carbohydrates, like bread or pasta, our body breaks these carbs down into glucose, a type of sugar. Glucose is the main fuel source, producing energy that keeps our cells and organs functioning.

Carbohydrates are the body's go-to source for quick energy. They're easily broken down into glucose and used immediately or stored for later use. This process works well for most people, especially when there's a balance between the carbs consumed and the body's energy needs.

The ketogenic diet changes this standard process by significantly reducing carbohydrate intake. When we cut down on carbs, our body's usual glucose supply runs low.

This decrease in glucose triggers a need for an alternative energy source, leading us to ketosis.

Ketosis is like a backup energy system. When the body can't get enough glucose, it looks for another fuel source. It finds this in fat.

The liver begins to convert fats into what are known as ketone bodies. These ketone bodies then travel through the bloodstream to various organs, supplying energy like glucose.

This switch from using glucose to using ketone bodies has several potential benefits. It helps in burning stored fats, leading to weight loss.

People often report having more stable energy levels and fewer ups and downs that can come with a carbohydrate diet.

The body adjusts to this new fuel source, a phase often called the "keto flu." During this period, some might feel tired or have headaches. But once the body adapts, many report feeling more energetic and mentally sharper.

The ability of our bodies to switch from glycolysis to ketosis is quite remarkable. It shows how adaptable our metabolism can be. The ketogenic diet leverages this adaptability, offering a different way to fuel our bodies, which can be especially beneficial as we age.

MYTHS AND REALITIES: DEBUNKING COMMON MISCONCEPTIONS ABOUT THE KETOGENIC DIET.

When it comes to the ketogenic diet, numerous myths and misconceptions can cloud understanding. It's essential to separate fact from fiction, especially for those considering this diet a lifestyle change. Let's address some common myths and present the realities.

A common misconception is that the ketogenic diet is akin to other high-protein, low-carb diets. In reality, the ketogenic diet is high in fat, moderate in protein, and very low in carbohydrates. The emphasis is on fats, which should comprise about 70-80% of daily calories, with protein at a moderate level. Consuming too much protein can hinder the process of ketosis.

Another myth is that the ketogenic diet is nutritionally deficient. Critics often claim it lacks essential vitamins and minerals in fruits, grains, and legumes. However, a ketogenic diet can be rich in nutrients when properly planned. It emphasizes various low-carbohydrate vegetables, healthy fats, and quality proteins, which can provide essential nutrients.

Some believe that the high-fat content of the ketogenic diet contributes to heart disease. However, research has shown that when the intake of fats is primarily from healthy sources (like avocados, nuts, and olive oil), the diet can improve heart health by reducing cholesterol levels. It's important to focus on healthy, unsaturated fats while avoiding trans fats.

There's a critical misunderstanding between ketosis, a safe and natural metabolic state induced by the ketogenic diet, and ketoacidosis, a dangerous medical condition mostly associated with type 1 diabetes. While ketosis results from controlled carbohydrate restriction, ketoacidosis occurs when there's a severe lack of insulin in the body, leading to extremely high levels of ketones, which can be life-threatening.

Many argue that the ketogenic diet is too restrictive and difficult to follow in the long term. However, with an increasing variety of keto-friendly foods and a better understanding of balancing the diet, many individuals find it sustainable and enjoyable. Personalization and planning are key to making it a long-term lifestyle choice.

2

BENEFITS AND CONSIDERATIONS FOR OVER 60

The ketogenic diet's role in enhancing longevity and preventing age-related diseases is particularly interesting to those over 60. This period of life brings about metabolic changes, and the diet's shift to fat as a primary energy source can be beneficial. By relying on ketones rather than glucose, the diet may boost energy levels and improve cellular efficiency, which are crucial for healthy aging.

Studies have indicated that this diet might extend longevity by reducing the body's metabolic stress. The lower production of reactive oxygen species and inflammation resulting from ketosis is linked to slowing down the aging process and reducing the risk of age-related diseases.

In the context of age-related disease prevention, the ketogenic diet is notable. As we grow older, our susceptibility to diseases like type 2 diabetes and heart conditions increases. The diet's ability to regulate blood sugar and improve cholesterol levels is key in lowering these risks. Additionally, its effectiveness in managing weight is particularly relevant for seniors, as obesity can exacerbate various age-related health issues. For older adults, adopting the ketogenic diet requires careful consideration of their specific nutritional needs. A balanced and nutrient-rich approach is essential. This might mean adjusting protein intake to maintain muscle mass and bone health, an important consideration for this diet plan.

Older adults should also be mindful of how the diet intersects with existing health conditions and medications. Consulting with healthcare providers is critical to ensure the diet complements overall health goals and is adapted to individual circumstances.

Regarding weight management and metabolism, the ketogenic diet offers a unique solution for older adults facing a natural slowdown in metabolism. Focusing on fat as a source of energy presents an effective weight control strategy, helping to counteract age-related metabolic decline.

Overall, the ketogenic diet emerges as a promising option for individuals over 60, not just for weight management but also as a means to enhance longevity and prevent certain age-related conditions. Customizing the diet to individual health needs, with professional guidance, is key to harnessing its full potential for improving health and wellness in later life.

CONSIDERATIONS ON HOW THE DIET MAY AFFECT AGE-RELATED CONDITIONS.

For those over 60 considering the ketogenic diet, it's essential to understand how it might interact with various age-related conditions.
This low-carb, high-fat diet has implications for different health aspects, making it a significant choice for seniors.
Cardiovascular health is a top concern in later years. The ketogenic diet can be beneficial here, improving blood sugar control and insulin sensitivity. However, focusing on healthy fats is crucial to maintain good cholesterol levels.
As we age, maintaining strong bones is vital. The ketogenic diet's influence on calcium and bone health warrants attention. Including keto-compatible calcium and vitamin D sources, like leafy greens and certain dairy products, can help support bone density.
The diet's shift in food types can also impact gut health, especially regarding fiber intake. Incorporating low-carb, high-fiber foods such as certain vegetables, nuts, and seeds is beneficial to support a healthy digestive system.
There is increasing interest in how the ketogenic diet may affect cognitive health, particularly regarding age-related decline. Some research points to potential neuroprotective benefits from the diet, likely due to ketones providing a steady energy source to the brain and their potential anti-inflammatory properties.
For many older adults, joint health and inflammation are ongoing concerns. The ketogenic diet has been linked to reduced inflammation, which could benefit those with joint issues. Still, individual responses vary, and closely monitoring how the diet affects these health aspects is important.

WEIGHT MANAGEMENT AND METABOLISM IN ADVANCED AGE.

Weight management and metabolism are critical factors in advanced age, and the ketogenic diet has specific implications in these areas.

Our metabolic rate naturally slows down as we age, making weight management more challenging.

This is where the ketogenic diet, with its unique approach to macronutrient balance, can be particularly beneficial.

The diet's high-fat, low-carbohydrate regime prompts the body to use fat as its primary energy source, which can aid in weight loss and metabolic regulation. This shift can be especially advantageous for older adults, as it aligns with the body's changing energy needs and metabolic capabilities.

Moreover, the ketogenic diet's impact on insulin sensitivity is another factor in effective weight management. By lowering carbohydrate intake, the diet helps regulate blood sugar levels, which can be particularly beneficial for seniors, who are more susceptible to insulin resistance. This regulation not only aids in weight control but also supports overall metabolic health.

It's also worth noting that the ketogenic diet can contribute to preserving muscle mass, an important aspect for older adults.

Muscle mass naturally declines with age, and maintaining it is crucial for sustaining a healthy metabolism and preventing sarcopenia, a condition characterized by significant loss of muscle mass and strength.

Incorporating the ketogenic diet into a lifestyle for those in their later years is a strategic approach to managing weight and maintaining metabolic health. It offers a way to adjust to the body's changing needs, potentially making weight management a more attainable goal.

As with any dietary change, especially at an older age, it's important to approach this transition mindfully and consider individual health conditions and nutritional needs.

3

NUTRITIONAL ASPECTS SPECIFIC TO OVER 60

For individuals over 60, addressing unique nutritional needs is key to maintaining health and well-being. Our bodies undergo various changes as we age, affecting how we process and utilize nutrients. Recognizing and adapting to these changes is crucial, especially when following a specific diet like the ketogenic diet.

One of the primary changes is a natural decline in metabolic rate, leading to reduced caloric needs.

However, the body's requirement for essential nutrients is still maintained. Therefore, focusing on nutrient-dense foods that provide vitamins, minerals, and other health-promoting compounds without excessive calories is important.

Protein needs often increase with age to maintain muscle mass, strength, and overall functionality. While moderate in protein, the ketogenic diet can still accommodate this need. Choosing high-quality protein sources like lean meats, fish, eggs, and dairy products that provide essential amino acids without excessive carbohydrates is important.

Bone density can decrease in later years, making calcium and vitamin D crucial for maintaining bone health. Keto-friendly calcium sources include leafy green vegetables, cheese, nuts, and seeds. Vitamin D is also vital and can be obtained through exposure to sunlight, supplements, and certain foods like fatty fish.

Fiber intake is often a concern in the ketogenic diet, as traditional high-fiber foods like grains and some fruits are restricted. However, including low-carb vegetables, nuts, and seeds can help maintain a healthy digestive system and promote regularity, which can sometimes be challenging for older adults.

Proper hydration is vital at any age, especially for seniors with a diminished sense of thirst. The ketogenic diet can also lead to changes in fluid and electrolyte balance. Drinking plenty of water and consuming foods rich in key electrolytes like potassium, magnesium, and sodium is important to maintain hydration and electrolyte balance.

Omega-3 fatty acids are important for heart and brain health. Sources like fatty fish (salmon, mackerel), flaxseeds, and walnuts are keto-friendly and can help meet these needs.

For those over 60, a well-planned ketogenic diet can meet these unique nutritional requirements while offering the benefits of this dietary approach. Focusing on various nutrient-rich foods within the ketogenic framework is essential to ensure a balanced diet that supports overall health and well-being in later life.

WHAT YOU CAN AND CANNOT EAT ON A KETOGENIC DIET.

Adopting a ketogenic diet involves understanding what foods to include and what to avoid to maintain ketosis, the metabolic state where the body burns fat for fuel instead of carbohydrates.

Foods to Include in a Ketogenic Diet

FATS AND OILS	Olive oil - Coconut oil - Avocado oil - Butter and ghee MCT oil - Fatty cuts of meat (preferably grass-fed) High-fat dairy products like cheese and heavy cream Nut oils (such as walnut or macadamia nut oil, in moderation)
PROTEIN	Grass-fed beef and lamb - Poultry - Pork Fish, especially fatty fish like salmon and mackerel - Seafood Eggs- Full-fat dairy products, like cheese and Greek yogurt
LOW-CARB VEGETABLES	Leafy greens (spinach, kale, swiss chard) Cruciferous vegetables (broccoli, cauliflower, Brussels sprouts) Zucchini - Bell peppers - Asparagus - Cucumbers - Celery - Eggplant Mushrooms - Garlic (in small amount

NUTS AND SEEDS	Almonds - Walnuts - Macadamia nuts - Pecans - Flaxseeds- Pumpkin seeds - Chia seeds - Sunflower seeds - Brazil nuts Hemp seeds

BERRIES	Raspberries - Blackberries - Strawberries Blueberries (in limited amounts) - Olives Lemons and limes (mostly used for flavoring in small amounts

AVOCADOS	Whole avocados Guacamole (without added sugars)

Foods to Avoid on a Ketogenic Diet:

SUGARY FOODS	Soda and sugary drinks - Candy and sweets - Pastries, cakes, and cookies - Ice cream - Fruit juices and smoothies with added sugar

GRAINS AND STARCHES	Bread and rolls - Pasta - Rice - Cereal Wheat-based products - Oats and oatmeal - Quinoa

FRUIT	Bananas - Apples - Oranges - Grapes - Pineapples Mangoes - Dried fruits

BEANS AND LEGUMES	Lentils - Chickpeas - Black beans Kidney beans - Peas

ROOT VEGETABLES	Potatoes and sweet potatoes - Carrots Beets - Parsnips

LOW-FAT PRODUCTS	Low-fat yogurts Low-fat dressings and sauces Diet sodas and drinks

ALCOHOLIC BEVERAGES	Beer Sweet wines Cocktails with sugary mixers

UNHEALTHY FATS	Processed vegetable oils (e.g., soybean oil, corn oil) Margarine Hydrogenated fats

TIPS FOR MAINTAINING MUSCLE MASS AND PREVENTING OSTEOPOROSIS.

Maintaining muscle mass and preventing osteoporosis is especially important as we age, and there are several practical ways to address these concerns, particularly for those following a ketogenic diet.

Starting with protein, it's the building block of muscle. While the ketogenic diet focuses on fats, ensuring enough high-quality protein is key. This means regularly including foods like lean meats, fish, eggs, and certain dairy products in your diet. The amount of protein you need depends on factors like age and activity level, but a good rule of thumb is to include a source of protein in each meal.

Resistance training is another crucial element. It's not just about lifting heavy weights; it's about engaging your muscles to promote growth and strength. This can be as simple as using resistance bands, doing bodyweight exercises, or even gardening activities involving lifting or pushing. Not only does this help with muscle mass, but it also strengthens your bones, which is vital for preventing osteoporosis.

Calcium is synonymous with bone health. The key is to incorporate calcium-rich, keto-friendly foods into your meals. Think leafy greens, almonds, cheese, and sesame seeds. These keep your bones strong and fit nicely into a ketogenic diet.

Vitamin D also plays a pivotal role, as it helps your body absorb calcium. While sunlight is a great source, you can also get vitamin D from fatty fish or egg yolks. Regular check-ups with your doctor can help you monitor your Vitamin D levels and ensure you get enough.

Then there's exercise. We're not just talking about hitting the gym. Activities like walking, light jogging, or even dancing can be great for your bones. They're weight-bearing exercises that help build bone density, reducing the risk of osteoporosis. Integrating flexibility and balance exercises like yoga can also be beneficial, helping to improve stability and reduce the risk of falls.

Remember magnesium and vitamin K2. Magnesium aids muscle and nerve function in nuts, seeds, and green veggies. Vitamin K2, which helps with bone metabolism, can be sourced from fermented foods and certain animal products.

These nutrients are often overshadowed but are just as important for muscle and bone health.

It's crucial to consume enough calories, a common mistake is eating too little which can lead to muscle loss, especially if you're active. Make sure your diet provides enough energy to support your lifestyle.

Hydration and maintaining electrolyte balance are equally important. Staying hydrated is essential for overall health, and electrolytes are vital for muscle function. They play a role in everything from muscle contractions to bone health, so include potassium-rich foods and consider a magnesium supplement if needed.

Incorporating these practices into your daily routine can greatly support muscle and bone health, significantly impacting your well-being, particularly as you follow a ketogenic diet in your later years.

4

GETTING STARTED

Getting started with the ketogenic diet involves both mental and physical preparation. This preparation is crucial, especially for those over 60, as it sets the foundation for a successful transition and long-term adherence to the diet.

Mental Preparation: Setting the Mindset

1. Understanding the Commitment: First and foremost, it's important to acknowledge that adopting the ketogenic diet is a lifestyle change, not just a temporary shift in eating habits. This understanding helps in mentally preparing for the adjustments ahead.

2. Educating Yourself: Learn as much as possible about the ketogenic diet. Understanding how it works, what foods to eat and avoid, and its potential benefits and challenges can equip you with the knowledge to make informed choices.

3. Setting Realistic Goals: Define clear, achievable goals. Whether it's weight loss, improved health markers, or enhanced well-being, having specific objectives can motivate you.

4. Developing a Positive Attitude: Approach the diet with a positive mindset. Embrace the changes as steps towards a healthier lifestyle. Remember, it's about making progress, not seeking perfection.

5. Seeking Support: Consider sharing your plan with friends, family, or a support group. Having others to discuss your journey, share tips, and offer encouragement can be incredibly helpful.

Physical Preparation: Priming the Body

1. Consulting with Healthcare Providers: It's important to consult with a healthcare provider before starting, especially for those with existing health conditions or taking medications. They can provide guidance tailored to your specific health needs.

2. Gradual Transition: Some may find it easier to gradually reduce carbohydrate intake than jumping straight into a strict ketogenic diet. This can help the body adjust more comfortably.

3. Pantry Overhaul: Prepare your kitchen. Remove high-carb foods not in line with the ketogenic diet and stock up on keto-friendly foods. Having the right foods at hand can make the transition smoother.

4. Planning Meals: Start planning your meals. This can help avoid the temptation of off-plan foods and make grocery shopping more efficient.

5. Monitoring Your Health: Pay attention to how your body responds during the initial phase. Keep track of changes in energy levels, mood, or other physical responses. Adjust as needed to ensure your body is getting the necessary nutrients.

6. Hydration and Electrolytes: Staying hydrated and maintaining electrolyte balance is crucial, especially during the initial phase when the body adjusts to a lower carb intake.

IDENTIFYING AND OVERCOMING COMMON CHALLENGES

Embarking on the ketogenic diet means facing and overcoming several common challenges, particularly when it involves altering long-standing eating habits. These habits, developed over a lifetime, can be deeply ingrained, making changes seem daunting. However, with the right strategies, these challenges can be successfully navigated.

Begin by identifying your current eating habits. Keep a food diary for a few days, noting what you eat, when, and why. This can help pinpoint triggers for unhealthy eating habits, such as emotional eating or snacking out of boredom.

Replace old habits with new, healthier ones. For example, if you habitually reach for sweet treats, try replacing them with keto-friendly snacks like nuts or cheese. It's about making small, manageable swaps initially, which can lead to bigger changes over time.

Meal planning is also a powerful tool. Plan your meals and snacks ahead of time, ensuring they fit within the ketogenic framework. This reduces the likelihood of impulsive, off-plan eating and eases the decision-making process about what to eat.

Cultivate a habit of mindful eating. This means eating slowly, savoring each bite, and paying attention to hunger and fullness cues. It can help prevent overeating and make meals more satisfying.

Social and family gatherings can pose a challenge, often involving non-keto foods. Plan by eating beforehand, bringing a keto-friendly dish to share, or suggesting restaurants that offer suitable options.

Be prepared for initial physical changes, such as the keto flu, as your body adapts to the ketogenic diet. Understanding that these are temporary can help you push through this phase. Staying hydrated and maintaining electrolyte balance is key during this time.

Finally, be patient with yourself. Changing long-standing habits doesn't happen overnight. There may be setbacks, but persistence is key. Celebrate small victories along the way to stay motivated.

By acknowledging these challenges and adopting strategies to address them, you can effectively transition to the ketogenic diet and make it a sustainable part of your lifestyle, leading to potential health benefits and improved well-being.

ADVICE ON CONSULTING HEALTH PROFESSIONALS BEFORE STARTING.

Consulting with health professionals before starting the ketogenic diet is a wise step, especially considering the unique needs and health considerations that come with age. This advice isn't just a formality; it's crucial to ensuring that your transition to a ketogenic lifestyle is safe, effective, and tailored to your individual health needs.

Firstly, it's important to understand that while the ketogenic diet has many potential benefits, it's a significant change from the typical diet, particularly regarding macronutrient distribution. This change can affect your body and health; some may need medical supervision, especially if you have existing health conditions or take medication.

For example, if you're on medication for diabetes or high blood pressure, entering a state of ketosis can alter how your body needs these medications. A healthcare professional can guide you on adjusting dosages as needed, which is crucial for avoiding potentially dangerous health complications.

Moreover, a medical professional, such as a doctor or dietitian, can help personalize the diet to your needs. They can consider nutritional requirements, pre-existing conditions like osteoporosis or kidney issues, and overall health goals. This personalized advice is invaluable because what works for one person may not be suitable for another, and it's essential to approach the ketogenic diet in a way that benefits your overall health.

A healthcare provider can also help set realistic and safe goals, whether they're related to weight loss, blood sugar control, or simply improving overall wellness. They can provide benchmarks and monitoring strategies to track your progress and make necessary adjustments.

Regular check-ups and consultations throughout your ketogenic journey can provide ongoing support and guidance. This can be especially helpful in monitoring your body's response to the diet, managing any side effects, and ensuring your nutritional needs are met.

Consulting with healthcare professionals is not just a step but an ongoing process that plays a pivotal role in your ketogenic journey. It ensures that your dietary choices align with your health requirements and goals, paving the way for a healthier, more balanced approach to eating and living, especially in your later years.

5

PERSONALIZING THE KETOGENIC DIET

Personalizing the ketogenic diet is key to making it a sustainable and enjoyable part of your lifestyle. This personalization involves adapting the diet to suit individual needs, tastes, and lifestyles, ensuring it's not just effective but also a pleasurable experience.

Each person's body is unique, and so are their nutritional requirements. Factors like age, gender, activity level, and existing health conditions play a significant role in determining your version of the ketogenic diet. For instance, if you're highly active, you might need more protein or a slightly higher carb intake to support your energy needs. Similarly, if you have certain dietary restrictions or preferences, like being vegetarian, you must find keto-friendly sources that align with these choices.

The beauty of the ketogenic diet is its versatility. A vast array of keto-friendly recipes and food options are available, allowing you to experiment and discover what you enjoy most. From savory dishes to keto desserts, the options are plentiful. Trying different recipes and foods can keep the diet interesting and more varied.

Your lifestyle should dictate the approach you take with the ketogenic diet. If you have a busy schedule, meal-prepping or simple keto recipes might be the most practical. On the other hand, if you enjoy cooking and have more time, experimenting with elaborate keto recipes can be a delightful part of your routine.

Paying attention to how your body responds to different aspects of the ketogenic diet is crucial. This means noticing how certain foods affect your energy levels, digestion, and overall well-being. It's about finding a balance that works best for you, which might mean tweaking the standard ketogenic macros to suit your body's responses better.

Pairing the ketogenic diet with an exercise routine that you enjoy can enhance its benefits. Whether it's walking, swimming, yoga, or weight training, find a form of physical activity that fits your preference and lifestyle.

Exercise complements the diet's effects on weight management and overall health and boosts mood and energy levels.

Regular check-ups with a healthcare provider can help fine-tune the diet to your specific health needs. This is especially important if you have underlying health conditions. Regular monitoring can ensure that the diet positively impacts your health markers like blood sugar, cholesterol levels, and blood pressure.

Be open to making adjustments. Personalizing the diet means it can evolve as your needs, tastes, and circumstances change. Flexibility and a willingness to adjust are key to maintaining a ketogenic lifestyle that is both beneficial and enjoyable.

STRATEGIES FOR MAINTAINING NUTRITIONAL BALANCE AND VARIETY IN THE DIET.

Navigating this diet successfully hinges on striking the right balance between adhering to its low-carb, high-fat principles and ensuring you get a wide range of nutrients. It's not just about limiting certain foods; it's about creatively embracing various options to make your meals nutritious and enjoyable.

Think about the bounty of low-carb vegetables available. There's a whole spectrum from leafy greens, offering an array of vitamins and minerals, to colorful bell peppers and zucchinis, each bringing unique flavors and nutritional profiles. These vegetables are more than just side dishes; they can be the stars of your meals, providing essential fiber and keeping your diet interesting and varied.

Proteins, too, deserve attention for their variety. Rotating between different protein sources like beef, poultry, fish, and eggs prevents boredom and ensures a mix of essential nutrients. Seafood, in particular, is a treasure trove of omega-3 fatty acids, crucial for heart and brain health. For those who lean towards plant-based diets, incorporating keto-friendly plant proteins adds another layer of variety.

The world of herbs and spices is vast and largely unexplored by many. These flavor powerhouses elevate the taste of your meals and pack in health benefits, from anti-inflammatory properties to aid in blood sugar control. They make it possible to enjoy the same foods differently by changing the seasoning.

Fats are central to the ketogenic diet; there's more to them than just butter and cheese. Alternating between different fat sources like plant-based oils, nuts, and fatty fish adds a nutritional dimension to the diet.

Each type of fat has its health benefits, and varying these sources can contribute to overall well-being.

Trying new recipes can be a delightful adventure. This cookbook is replete with keto-friendly recipes that can introduce you to new ways of cooking and eating.

From gourmet dishes to simple, everyday meals, the options are endless and can make your keto journey exciting.

While focusing on macronutrients, keep sight of the micronutrients. Supplements are sometimes necessary to fill nutritional gaps, especially if certain food groups are limited. Consulting with a healthcare provider for personalized supplement advice can be helpful.

MONITORING AND ADJUSTING THE DIET OVER TIME.

As you progress with the ketogenic diet, monitoring and making adjustments over time is integral to the journey. It's not just about setting a plan and sticking to it rigidly; it's about evolving and adapting the plan as you go along based on your body's responses and changing needs.

Continuous monitoring involves keeping an eye on several key aspects. Firstly, it's about tracking your dietary intake. While initially, it might involve closely counting carbs and fats, it becomes more intuitive over time. However, it's still beneficial to periodically check in on your eating patterns to ensure they align with your goals and nutritional needs.

Another vital aspect is listening to your body's feedback. How do you feel overall? Are you experiencing sustained energy levels, or do you find yourself feeling fatigued? How is your digestion responding to the diet? Are you noticing weight and body composition changes that reflect your goals? These questions are important touchpoints. They help you gauge whether your current approach is working or adjustments are needed.

Regular health check-ups are also key in monitoring your progress. This can mean getting blood work done to see how the diet is affecting your cholesterol levels, blood sugar, and other key health markers. Based on these results, you might need to tweak your diet – maybe you need more fiber, less saturated fat, or additional supplements.

Adjustments to the diet can also come from lifestyle or health status changes. For example, if you become more active, you should increase your protein intake or adjust your calorie consumption. Likewise, changes in health conditions might necessitate dietary modifications.

The beauty of the ketogenic diet lies in its flexibility. It's not a one-size-fits-all approach but a customizable plan that can change as you do. Periodic reassessment and adjustment of the diet ensure that it meets your needs and goals, providing optimal benefits for your health and well-being.

6

SIDE EFFECTS AND HOW TO MANAGE THEM

Transitioning to the ketogenic diet involves a significant shift in your body's primary energy source, and this change can sometimes lead to a range of side effects, particularly in the initial stages.

Being aware of these potential side effects and knowing how to manage them can make your switch to the ketogenic lifestyle more comfortable and sustainable.

Keto Flu

One of the most common experiences when starting the ketogenic diet is the "keto flu."

This term refers to symptoms that may occur as your body adjusts from burning glucose to burning fat for energy.

Symptoms can include fatigue, headaches, dizziness, irritability, nausea, and difficulty concentrating.

How to Manage: Staying hydrated and increasing salt intake can help alleviate these symptoms. Drinking bone broth or adding extra salt to your food can be beneficial. Getting adequate sleep and moderate physical activity during this adjustment period is also important.

Digestive Issues

Changes in diet can impact digestion. Some people may experience constipation or diarrhea when they first start a ketogenic diet.

How to Manage: To combat constipation, ensure you're consuming enough fiber from low-carb vegetables and possibly supplementing with magnesium. For diarrhea, it often helps to review your diet for any potential intolerant foods, like dairy or artificial sweeteners.

Muscle Cramps and Spasms

Reductions in insulin levels on a ketogenic diet can lead to a loss of electrolytes, which can cause muscle cramps or spasms.

How to Manage: Keeping up with electrolyte intake is crucial. This can involve consuming foods rich in potassium, magnesium, and sodium or taking electrolyte supplements if necessary.

Bad Breath

Some people on a ketogenic diet may experience bad breath, often described as fruity or slightly sweet. This is due to the increased production of acetone, a ketone type that is sometimes released in the breath.

How to Manage: Regular brushing and staying hydrated can help, and this side effect usually diminishes as your body becomes more adapted to ketosis.

Changes in Energy and Sleep Patterns

Initial energy levels and sleep pattern changes are common as your body adapts. You might experience fatigue or have difficulty sleeping.

How to Manage: This typically improves as your body gets used to using ketones for energy. In the meantime, practicing good sleep hygiene and ensuring a balanced diet can help. If fatigue persists, check in with your doctor to rule out other causes.

Hunger and Cravings

Early on, you might experience increased hunger or cravings, particularly for carbs, as your body adjusts to reduced carbohydrate intake.

How to Manage: Eating regularly and choosing satiating foods high in fats and proteins can help keep hunger at bay. Also, allowing yourself time to adapt and staying busy can distract from cravings.

It's important to remember that these side effects are often temporary and tend to resolve as your body becomes more accustomed to using fat for fuel. Listening to your body and making adjustments, such as tweaking your diet or incorporating supplements, can go a long way in managing these side effects effectively.

While many of the side effects associated with starting the ketogenic diet are typically short-lived and can often be managed with simple dietary adjustments, there are certain situations where it's essential to seek medical advice if you experience persistent symptoms that significantly impact your daily life or have any concerns about your health. In contrast, it's important to consult a doctor on the diet.

Specifically, suppose symptoms like extreme fatigue, persistent digestive issues, severe muscle cramps, or other unusual health changes continue beyond the initial adjustment period. In that case, a healthcare professional can help determine whether these are normal side effects or signs of a more serious underlying issue. This is particularly important for individuals with pre-existing health conditions, such as heart or kidney diseases, or those taking medications that can be affected by dietary changes.

Remember, a healthcare provider can offer personalized guidance based on your health profile and ensure that your transition to and maintenance of the ketogenic diet is safe and beneficial for your overall health and well-being. Their expertise can be invaluable in making the ketogenic lifestyle a positive and healthy experience.

20 KETO
Breakfast
RECIPES

CLASSIC KETO OMELETTE

The Classic Keto Omelette is a timeless breakfast dish that is not only delicious but also perfectly aligns with the ketogenic diet principles. Packed with protein and healthy fats, it's a satisfying start to the day.

Ingredients

- 8 large eggs
- 1/2 cup heavy cream
- Salt and pepper, to taste
- 2 tablespoons unsalted butter
- 1 cup shredded cheddar cheese
- 1/2 cup diced bell peppers
- 1/2 cup chopped spinach
- 1/4 cup finely diced onion

Preparation Steps

- In a large bowl, whisk together the eggs, heavy cream, salt, and pepper until well combined and fluffy.
- Heat a non-stick skillet over medium heat and melt 1 tablespoon of butter.
- Pour in a quarter of the egg mixture, tilting the pan to spread it evenly. Cook for 2 minutes or until the bottom starts to set.
- Sprinkle a quarter each of the cheese, bell peppers, spinach, and onion over the omelette.
- Gently fold the omelette in half and cook for another 2-3 minutes, or until the cheese melts and the eggs are cooked to your liking.
- Repeat the process with the remaining ingredients to make four omelettes in total.
- Serve each omelette warm.

Preparation Time : 10 min

Cook Time : 10 min

Total Time: 20 min

Serving : 4

NUTRITIONAL INFO (per serving)

Calories: 320

Total Fat: 26g

Protein: 18g

Total Carbohydrates: 4g

Net Carbs: 2g

ALLERGEN
Contains dairy (cheese, heavy cream) and eggs.

AVOCADO AND EGG SALAD

This Avocado and Egg Salad is a refreshing and nutritious dish, perfect for a keto-friendly breakfast. The combination of creamy avocado and protein-rich eggs makes it a fulfilling and heart-healthy option.

Ingredients

- 4 large hard-boiled eggs, peeled and chopped
- 2 ripe avocados, diced
- 1/4 cup mayonnaise, preferably sugar-free
- 2 tablespoons fresh lemon juice
- Salt and pepper, to taste
- 2 tablespoons chopped fresh chives or green onions (optional)
- 1/4 teaspoon paprika (optional)

Preparation Steps

- In a medium-sized bowl, gently mix the chopped hard-boiled eggs and diced avocados.
- In a small bowl, whisk together the mayonnaise and lemon juice until smooth. Add salt and pepper to taste.
- Pour the mayonnaise mixture over the eggs and avocados. Gently toss to coat evenly.
- If using, sprinkle the salad with chopped chives or green onions and paprika for extra flavor and color.
- Serve immediately, or refrigerate for up to an hour before serving for flavors to meld.

🍲	**Preparation Time : 15 min**
🥄	**Cook Time : 10 min**
🕐	**Total Time: 25 min**
🍴	**Serving : 4**

NUTRITIONAL INFO (per serving)

Calories: 290

Total Fat: 25g

Protein: 9g

Total Carbohydrates: 8g

Net Carbs: 2g

ALLERGEN
Contains eggs. May contain dairy, depending on the type of mayonnaise used.

GREEK YOGURT WITH NUTS AND BERRIES

Greek Yogurt with Nuts and Berries is a delightful and easy-to-prepare ketogenic breakfast option. Combining the creamy texture of Greek yogurt with the crunchiness of nuts and the sweetness of berries, it offers a perfect balance of flavors and textures, along with essential nutrients to kickstart your day.

Ingredients

- 2 cups full-fat Greek yogurt
- 1/2 cup mixed berries (such as raspberries, blackberries, and strawberries)
- 1/4 cup almonds, roughly chopped
- 1/4 cup walnuts, roughly chopped
- Optional: a drizzle of sugar-free sweetener or a sprinkle of cinnamon for added flavor

Preparation Steps

- Divide the Greek yogurt evenly into four serving bowls.
- Top each bowl of yogurt with an equal portion of the mixed berries.
- Sprinkle the chopped almonds and walnuts over the yogurt and berries.
- If desired, add a light drizzle of sugar-free sweetener or a sprinkle of cinnamon for extra flavor.
- Serve immediately and enjoy a refreshing, nutrient-packed breakfast.

	Preparation Time : 5 min
	Cook Time : 0 min
	Total Time: 5 min
	Serving : 4

NUTRITIONAL INFO (per serving)

Calories: 180

Total Fat: 10g

Protein: 12g

Total Carbohydrates: 8g

Net Carbs: 6g

ALLERGEN
Contains Dairy (yogurt), Nuts

CHEESY SPINACH BAKED EGGS

Cheesy Spinach Baked Eggs is a nutritious and comforting breakfast dish, perfect for a keto-friendly start to the day. Combining the goodness of spinach with the richness of cheese and the heartiness of baked eggs, this dish is both satisfying and healthful.

Ingredients

- 4 cups fresh spinach, roughly chopped
- 4 large eggs
- 1/2 cup shredded cheddar cheese
- 1/4 cup heavy cream
- 2 tablespoons unsalted butter
- Salt and pepper, to taste
- Optional: a pinch of nutmeg or garlic powder for extra flavor

Preparation Steps

- Preheat the oven to 375°F (190°C).
- In a skillet, melt the butter over medium heat and sauté the spinach until it wilts, about 2-3 minutes. Season with salt, pepper, and optional nutmeg or garlic powder.
- Divide the sautéed spinach evenly into four ramekins or a small baking dish.
- Crack an egg on top of the spinach in each ramekin.
- Drizzle the heavy cream evenly over each egg and top with the shredded cheddar cheese.
- Place the ramekins on a baking tray and bake in the preheated oven for 12-15 minutes, or until the egg whites are set but yolks are still runny.
- Remove from the oven, let it cool for a couple of minutes, and serve warm.

🥣	**Preparation Time : 10 min**
🥄	**Cook Time : 15 min**
🕐	**Total Time: 25 min**
🍴	**Serving : 4**

NUTRITIONAL INFO (per serving)

Calories: 220

Total Fat: 18g

Protein: 13g

Total Carbohydrates: 3g

Net Carbs: 2g

ALLERGEN
Contains Eggs, Dairy (cheese)

KETO CAULIFLOWER HASH BROWNS

Keto Cauliflower Hash Browns offer a delicious low-carb alternative to traditional hash browns. Made with grated cauliflower, they provide a crispy, savory breakfast option that fits perfectly into a ketogenic lifestyle. These hash browns are not only tasty but also a great way to incorporate more vegetables into your morning routine.

Ingredients

- 1 medium head of cauliflower, grated
- 1/2 cup shredded cheddar cheese
- 1 large egg, beaten
- 2 tablespoons almond flour
- 1/2 teaspoon garlic powder
- Salt and pepper, to taste
- 2-3 tablespoons olive oil for frying

Preparation Steps

- Place the grated cauliflower in a clean kitchen towel and squeeze out as much moisture as possible.
- In a large bowl, mix the drained cauliflower, cheddar cheese, beaten egg, almond flour, garlic powder, salt, and pepper until well combined.
- Heat olive oil in a non-stick skillet over medium heat.
- Scoop portions of the cauliflower mixture into the skillet, flattening them into hash brown shapes with a spatula.
- Cook for about 4-5 minutes on each side or until they are golden brown and crispy.
- Remove from the skillet and drain on paper towels to remove excess oil.
- Serve hot as a side or with your favorite keto-friendly toppings.

🥣	**Preparation Time : 15 min**
🥄	**Cook Time : 10 min**
🕐	**Total Time: 25 min**
🍴	**Serving : 4**

NUTRITIONAL INFO (per serving)

Calories: 180

Total Fat: 14g

Protein: 7g

Total Carbohydrates: 6g

Net Carbs: 3g

ALLERGEN
Contains Eggs, Dairy (cheese)

ALMOND FLOUR PANCAKES

Almond Flour Pancakes offer a delightful, low-carb alternative for those on a ketogenic diet who crave the comfort of a classic pancake. These pancakes are light, fluffy, and full of flavor, making them a perfect breakfast treat that doesn't compromise your dietary goals.

Ingredients

- 1 1/2 cups almond flour
- 3 large eggs
- 1/4 cup unsweetened almond milk
- 1 tablespoon granulated erythritol or another sugar-free sweetener
- 1 teaspoon baking powder
- 1/2 teaspoon vanilla extract
- Pinch of salt
- Butter or coconut oil for frying

Preparation Steps

- In a large bowl, combine the almond flour, baking powder, erythritol, and a pinch of salt.
- In another bowl, whisk together the eggs, almond milk, and vanilla extract.
- Gradually mix the wet ingredients into the dry ingredients until a smooth batter forms.
- Heat a non-stick skillet over medium heat and add a small amount of butter or coconut oil.
- Pour 1/4 cup of batter for each pancake onto the skillet. Cook for 2-3 minutes until bubbles form on the surface, then flip and cook for an additional 2-3 minutes until golden brown.
- Repeat with the remaining batter, adding more butter or oil as needed.
- Serve warm with your choice of keto-friendly toppings, such as sugar-free syrup, whipped cream, or fresh berries.

Preparation Time : 10 min

Cook Time : 15 min

Total Time: 25 min

Serving : 4

NUTRITIONAL INFO (per serving)

Calories: 280

Total Fat: 23g

Protein: 12g

Total Carbohydrates: 9g

Net Carbs: 4g

ALLERGEN
Contains Eggs, Nuts (almond flour), Dairy (if using butter or dairy toppings)

COCONUT CHIA PUDDING

Coconut Chia Pudding is a simple, yet delicious ketogenic breakfast option that combines the rich, creamy texture of coconut milk with the health benefits of chia seeds. This dish is not only easy to prepare but also offers a delightful way to start your day with a nutrient-packed meal.

Ingredients

- 1 can (13.5 oz) full-fat coconut milk
- 1/4 cup chia seeds
- 1 tablespoon sugar-free sweetener (like erythritol or stevia)
- 1/2 teaspoon vanilla extract
- Optional toppings: unsweetened shredded coconut, a few berries, or a sprinkle of cinnamon

Preparation Steps

- In a mixing bowl, whisk together the coconut milk, chia seeds, sugar-free sweetener, and vanilla extract until well combined.
- Divide the mixture evenly into four serving glasses or bowls.
- Cover and refrigerate overnight, or for at least 4 hours, until the pudding has thickened and the chia seeds have absorbed the liquid.
- Before serving, stir the pudding to ensure an even texture.
- Garnish with optional toppings like unsweetened shredded coconut, a few berries, or a sprinkle of cinnamon for added flavor.
- Serve chilled.

Preparation Time : 5 min (plus overnight for soaking)

Cook Time : 0 min

Total Time: 5 min (plus soaking time)

Serving : 4

NUTRITIONAL INFO (per serving)

Calories: 250

Total Fat: 22g

Protein: 4g

Total Carbohydrates: 12g

Net Carbs: 3g

ALLERGEN
Contains Nuts (coconut)

KETO BREAKFAST SMOOTHIE

This Keto Breakfast Smoothie is a refreshing and energizing way to start your day while sticking to your ketogenic diet. Combining healthy fats, protein, and low-carb fruits, this smoothie is not only delicious but also nutritionally balanced, keeping you satisfied throughout the morning.

Ingredients

- 2 cups unsweetened almond milk
- 1 cup spinach leaves
- 1/2 avocado, peeled and pitted
- 1/4 cup frozen raspberries or strawberries
- 1/4 cup full-fat Greek yogurt
- 2 tablespoons almond butter
- 1 tablespoon chia seeds
- 1 tablespoon sugar-free sweetener (like erythritol or stevia)
- 1/2 teaspoon vanilla extract
- Ice cubes (optional)

Preparation Steps

- In a blender, combine the almond milk, spinach, avocado, frozen berries, Greek yogurt, almond butter, chia seeds, sweetener, and vanilla extract.
- Blend on high until smooth and creamy. If the smoothie is too thick, you can add a bit more almond milk to reach your desired consistency.
- If you prefer a colder smoothie, add a handful of ice cubes and blend again until smooth.
- Once blended to perfection, pour the smoothie into four glasses.
- Serve immediately for a fresh and revitalizing keto-friendly breakfast.

	Preparation Time : 5 min
	Cook Time : 0 min
	Total Time: 5 min
	Serving : 4

NUTRITIONAL INFO (per serving)

Calories: 180

Total Fat: 14g

Protein: 6g

Total Carbohydrates: 8g

Net Carbs: 4g

ALLERGEN
- Contains Dairy (if using dairy milk or yogurt), Nuts (if using nut milk or nut butter - almond)

KETO SPINACH AND FETA BREAKFAST MUFFINS

Keto Spinach and Feta Breakfast Muffins are a savory and delightful way to start your day. Packed with nutritious spinach, creamy feta cheese, and eggs, these muffins are perfect for a quick and satisfying keto-friendly breakfast. They're not only delicious but also portable, making them ideal for busy mornings or on-the-go snacking.

Ingredients

- 4 large eggs
- 1 cup fresh spinach, chopped
- 1/2 cup feta cheese, crumbled
- 1/4 cup almond flour
- 1/4 cup heavy cream
- 2 tablespoons olive oil
- 1/2 teaspoon baking powder
- Salt and pepper, to taste
- Optional: 1/4 cup diced bell peppers or onions

Preparation Steps

- Preheat your oven to 350°F (175°C). Grease a 6-cup muffin tin or line it with silicone muffin cups.
- In a large bowl, whisk together the eggs, heavy cream, and olive oil until well combined.
- Stir in the almond flour, baking powder, salt, and pepper. Mix until just combined.
- Fold in the chopped spinach, crumbled feta cheese, and optional diced bell peppers or onions.
- Evenly distribute the mixture into the prepared muffin cups.
- Bake in the preheated oven for 20 minutes, or until the muffins are set and lightly golden on top.
- Remove from the oven and let them cool for a few minutes before removing them from the muffin tin.
- Serve the Keto Spinach and Feta Breakfast Muffins warm.

	Preparation Time : 15 min
	Cook Time : 20 min
	Total Time: 35 min
	Serving : 4

NUTRITIONAL INFO (per serving)

Calories: 180

Total Fat: 14g

Protein: 9g

Total Carbohydrates: 3g

Net Carbs: 2g

ALLERGEN
Contains dairy (feta cheese), eggs, and nuts (almond flour)

ZUCCHINI FRITTERS

Zucchini Fritters are a delightful and nutritious addition to a ketogenic breakfast menu. Made with fresh zucchini, these fritters are crispy on the outside and tender on the inside, offering a delicious way to enjoy vegetables in the morning. They're easy to prepare and can be a versatile base for various toppings.

Ingredients

- 2 medium zucchinis, grated
- 2 large eggs, beaten
- 1/2 cup almond flour
- 1/2 cup grated Parmesan cheese
- 2 cloves garlic, minced
- Salt and pepper, to taste
- 1/4 cup olive oil for frying
- Optional: a pinch of dried herbs like basil or oregano

Preparation Steps

- Place the grated zucchini in a colander and sprinkle with a little salt. Let it sit for 10 minutes to draw out moisture. Squeeze the excess water from the zucchini using a clean kitchen towel.
- In a mixing bowl, combine the drained zucchini, beaten eggs, almond flour, grated Parmesan, minced garlic, and optional dried herbs. Season with salt and pepper.
- Heat olive oil in a skillet over medium heat.
- Scoop about 2 tablespoons of the zucchini mixture per fritter into the skillet. Flatten them slightly with the back of a spoon to form fritters.
- Fry for about 4-5 minutes on each side or until golden brown and crispy.
- Transfer the fritters to a plate lined with paper towels to drain any excess oil.
- Serve warm, either plain or with your favorite keto-friendly dipping sauce.

🥣	**Preparation Time : 15 min**
🔪	**Cook Time : 10 min**
🕐	**Total Time: 25 min**
🍴	**Serving : 4**

NUTRITIONAL INFO (per serving)

Calories: 230

Total Fat: 19g

Protein: 10g

Total Carbohydrates: 6g

Net Carbs: 3g

ALLERGEN
Contains Eggs, Dairy (cheese)

SMOKED SALMON AND CREAM CHEESE ROLL-UPS

Smoked Salmon and Cream Cheese Roll-Ups are an elegant, no-cook breakfast option perfect for the ketogenic diet. These roll-ups combine the rich flavor of smoked salmon with the creamy texture of cream cheese, creating a delicious and sophisticated dish that's also incredibly easy to prepare.

Ingredients

- 8 slices of smoked salmon
- 4 oz cream cheese, softened
- 1 tablespoon fresh dill, chopped
- 1/4 cup cucumber, thinly sliced
- 1 tablespoon capers (optional)
- Salt and pepper to taste
- Lemon wedges for serving (optional)

Preparation Steps

- Lay out the smoked salmon slices on a flat surface.
- In a small bowl, mix the cream cheese with chopped dill, salt, and pepper until smooth and spreadable.
- Spread a thin layer of the cream cheese mixture over each slice of smoked salmon.
- Place a few slices of cucumber and a few capers, if using, at one end of each salmon slice.
- Carefully roll up the salmon slices, starting from the end with the cucumber.
- Cut each roll-up in half, if desired, and secure with a toothpick.
- Serve the roll-ups with lemon wedges on the side for a refreshing zest.

	Preparation Time : 1o min
	Cook Time : 0 min
	Total Time: 10 min
	Serving : 4

NUTRITIONAL INFO (per serving)

Calories: 150

Total Fat: 11g

Protein: 12g

Total Carbohydrates: 2g

Net Carbs: 1g

ALLERGEN
Contains Fish (salmon), Dairy (cream cheese)

BACON AND EGG CUPS

Bacon and Egg Cups are a delightful and convenient keto-friendly breakfast option. These little cups combine the savory taste of bacon with the richness of eggs, baked together to perfection. They're not only delicious but also perfectly portioned, making them a great choice for a quick and satisfying breakfast.

Ingredients

- 8 slices of bacon
- 8 large eggs
- Salt and pepper, to taste
- Optional toppings: shredded cheese, diced bell peppers, or chopped herbs (like chives or parsley)

Preparation Steps

- Preheat your oven to 375°F (190°C). Grease a muffin tin with a little oil or butter.
- Cook the bacon slices in a skillet over medium heat until they are partially cooked but still pliable, about 3-4 minutes. Drain on paper towels.
- Line each muffin cup with a slice of bacon, forming a ring around the sides.
- Crack an egg into each bacon-lined cup. Season with salt and pepper.
- Add optional toppings like shredded cheese or diced bell peppers if desired.
- Bake in the preheated oven for 12-15 minutes, or until the egg whites are set but the yolks are still slightly runny.
- Remove from the oven and let them cool for a couple of minutes. Use a spoon or knife to gently lift each bacon and egg cup out of the muffin tin.
- Serve warm.

 Preparation Time : 10 min

 Cook Time : 15 min

 Total Time: 25 min

Serving : 4 (2 cups per serving)

NUTRITIONAL INFO (per serving)

Calories: 280

Total Fat: 22g

Protein: 20g

Total Carbohydrates: 1g

Net Carbs: 1g

ALLERGEN
Contains Eggs, Pork (bacon)

HAM AND CHEESE STUFFED MUSHROOMS

Ham and Cheese Stuffed Mushrooms are a savory and delightful breakfast choice for those on a ketogenic diet. Combining the earthy flavors of mushrooms with the richness of cheese and the smoky taste of ham, these stuffed mushrooms are not only delicious but also easy to prepare, making them perfect for a satisfying keto breakfast or brunch.

Ingredients

- 16 large button mushrooms, stems removed
- 1/2 cup cooked ham, finely chopped
- 1/2 cup cream cheese, softened
- 1/4 cup grated Parmesan cheese
- 1/4 cup shredded mozzarella cheese
- 1 clove garlic, minced
- Salt and pepper, to taste
- 1 tablespoon olive oil
- Optional: chopped parsley for garnish

Preparation Steps

- Preheat your oven to 350°F (175°C). Line a baking sheet with parchment paper.
- Gently clean the mushrooms with a damp paper towel and remove the stems.
- In a bowl, mix together the ham, cream cheese, Parmesan cheese, mozzarella cheese, minced garlic, salt, and pepper.
- Fill each mushroom cap with the ham and cheese mixture, pressing down lightly to secure the filling.
- Arrange the stuffed mushrooms on the prepared baking sheet.
- Lightly brush the tops of the mushrooms with olive oil.
- Bake in the preheated oven for 18-20 minutes, or until the mushrooms are tender and the cheese is melted and lightly golden.
- Garnish with chopped parsley if desired before serving.

Preparation Time : 15 min

Cook Time : 20 min

Total Time: 35 min

Serving : 4

NUTRITIONAL INFO (per serving)

Calories: 210

Total Fat: 16g

Protein: 14g

Total Carbohydrates: 4g

Net Carbs: 3g

ALLERGEN
Contains Dairy (cheese), Pork (ham)

KETO BREAKFAST PORRIDGE

Keto Breakfast 'Porridge' is a comforting and warm alternative to traditional oat-based porridge, aligning perfectly with the ketogenic lifestyle. Made with a blend of nutritious seeds and creamy coconut milk, this porridge provides a cozy and satisfying start to the day, packed with fiber and healthy fats.

Ingredients

- 1/4 cup chia seeds
- 1/4 cup flaxseeds, ground
- 1/4 cup hemp seeds
- 1 cup unsweetened coconut milk (can substitute with almond milk)
- 1/2 teaspoon cinnamon
- 1 tablespoon sugar-free sweetener (like erythritol or stevia)
- Optional toppings: unsweetened shredded coconut, sliced almonds, fresh berries, or a dollop of almond butter

Preparation Steps

- In a saucepan, combine chia seeds, ground flaxseeds, hemp seeds, coconut milk, cinnamon, and sugar-free sweetener.
- Bring the mixture to a low simmer over medium heat, stirring frequently to prevent sticking.
- Cook for 8-10 minutes, or until the mixture thickens to a porridge-like consistency.
- Remove from heat and let it cool slightly. The porridge will continue to thicken as it cools.
- Divide the porridge into four servings and add your choice of optional toppings, such as shredded coconut, sliced almonds, fresh berries, or a dollop of almond butter.
- Serve warm and enjoy a hearty, keto-friendly breakfast.

🥣	**Preparation Time : 5 min**
🍳	**Cook Time : 10 min**
🕐	**Total Time: 15 min**
🍴	**Serving : 4**

NUTRITIONAL INFO (per serving)

Calories: 220

Total Fat: 18g

Protein: 10g

Total Carbohydrates: 9g

Net Carbs: 3g

ALLERGEN
Contains Nuts (if using nut-based milk or nuts as ingredients)

SAUSAGE AND PEPPER SKILLET

The Sausage and Pepper Skillet is a hearty and flavorful breakfast dish that fits perfectly into a ketogenic diet. Combining savory sausages with colorful bell peppers and onions, this skillet meal is not only satisfying but also a great way to start your day with a boost of protein and essential nutrients.

Ingredients

- 4 large sausages (preferably a keto-friendly variety, like Italian or breakfast sausages)
- 2 bell peppers, sliced (choose different colors for variety)
- 1 medium onion, sliced
- 2 tablespoons olive oil
- Salt and pepper to taste
- Optional: crushed red pepper flakes for a spicy kick

Preparation Steps

- Heat a large skillet over medium heat and add the olive oil.
- Add the sausages to the skillet and cook until browned on all sides and cooked through, about 10 minutes. Remove the sausages and set them aside.
- In the same skillet, add the sliced bell peppers and onion. Season with salt, pepper, and optional red pepper flakes.
- Sauté the vegetables until they are soft and slightly caramelized, about 10 minutes.
- Slice the cooked sausages and return them to the skillet with the vegetables. Stir to combine and heat through for a couple of minutes.
- Taste and adjust seasoning as needed.
- Serve the sausage and pepper skillet hot, divided into four portions.

🥣	**Preparation Time : 10 min**
🥄	**Cook Time : 20 min**
🕐	**Total Time: 30 min**
✗	**Serving : 4**

NUTRITIONAL INFO (per serving)

Calories: 350

Total Fat: 25g

Protein: 22g

Total Carbohydrates: 8g

Net Carbs: 6g

ALLERGEN
Contains Pork (sausage)

KETO VEGGIE BREAKFAST SCRAMBLE

The Keto Veggie Breakfast Scramble is a vibrant and nutritious way to start your day. Packed with fresh vegetables and fluffy scrambled eggs, this dish is not only colorful and flavorful but also aligns perfectly with a ketogenic lifestyle. It's a fantastic breakfast choice for those seeking a filling and healthy meal to kickstart their morning.

Ingredients

- 8 large eggs
- 1/4 cup heavy cream
- Salt and pepper, to taste
- 2 tablespoons butter or olive oil
- 1/2 cup diced bell peppers (mix of colors)
- 1/4 cup chopped spinach
- 1/4 cup diced zucchini
- 1/4 cup chopped mushrooms
- 1/2 cup shredded cheddar cheese
- Optional: chopped fresh herbs such as parsley or chives for garnish

Preparation Steps

- In a bowl, whisk together the eggs, heavy cream, salt, and pepper until well combined and fluffy.
- Heat butter or olive oil in a large skillet over medium heat.
- Add the bell peppers, zucchini, and mushrooms to the skillet. Sauté until the vegetables are tender, about 5 minutes.
- Pour the egg mixture over the vegetables. Let it sit for a moment before gently stirring with a spatula, forming soft curds.
- Just before the eggs are fully set, stir in the chopped spinach and shredded cheddar cheese. Cook for an additional minute or until the cheese is melted and the eggs are cooked to your liking.
- Remove from heat. Garnish with optional chopped herbs.
- Serve the scramble hot, divided evenly among four plates.

Preparation Time : 10 min	
Cook Time : 10 min	
Total Time: 20 min	
Serving : 4	

NUTRITIONAL INFO (per serving)

Calories: 320

Total Fat: 25g

Protein: 20g

Total Carbohydrates: 5g

Net Carbs: 3g

ALLERGEN
Contains Eggs, Dairy (cheese)

FLAXSEED KETO WRAPS

Flaxseed Keto Wraps are a fantastic, low-carb alternative to traditional wraps, perfect for those on a ketogenic diet. Made primarily with flaxseeds, these wraps are not only nutritious, packed with fiber and omega-3 fatty acids, but also incredibly versatile and can be filled with a variety of ingredients for a delicious and satisfying meal.

Ingredients

- 1 cup ground flaxseed
- 1/4 teaspoon baking powder
- 1/4 teaspoon salt
- 1/2 teaspoon garlic powder (optional)
- 1 cup boiling water
- 1 tablespoon olive oil or coconut oil for cooking

Preparation Steps

- In a mixing bowl, combine the ground flaxseed, baking powder, salt, and garlic powder (if using).
- Add the boiling water to the dry ingredients and stir until a thick dough forms. Let the dough rest for 5 minutes to thicken further.
- Divide the dough into four equal parts. Roll each portion into a ball.
- Place one dough ball between two sheets of parchment paper and roll it out into a thin, round wrap shape.
- Heat a skillet over medium heat and add a bit of olive oil or coconut oil.
- Carefully transfer the rolled-out wrap to the skillet and cook for about 2-3 minutes on each side, or until it is slightly browned and firm.
- Repeat with the remaining dough balls.
- Once cooked, fill the wraps with your choice of keto-friendly fillings such as cooked meats, cheese, avocado, or leafy greens.

Preparation Time : 10 min

Cook Time : 5 minutes per wrap

Total Time: 35 min (for 4 wraps)

Serving : 4 (4 wraps)

NUTRITIONAL INFO (per serving)

Calories: 200

Total Fat: 15g

Protein: 7g

Total Carbohydrates: 10g

Net Carbs: 3g

ALLERGEN
Contains No major allergens unless filling contains allergens

CINNAMON FLAVORED KETO YOGURT PARFAIT

The Cinnamon Flavored Keto Yogurt Parfait combines the creamy texture of Greek yogurt with the warm spice of cinnamon, creating a delightful and easy-to-make breakfast. This parfait is not only pleasing to the palate but also aligns perfectly with a ketogenic diet, offering a good balance of protein, healthy fats, and low-carb sweetness.

Ingredients

- 2 cups full-fat Greek yogurt
- 2 teaspoons ground cinnamon
- Sugar-free sweetener equivalent to 2 tablespoons of sugar (like erythritol or stevia)
- 1 teaspoon vanilla extract
- 1/2 cup almonds, chopped
- 1/2 cup unsweetened coconut flakes
- Optional: a few berries for topping (like raspberries or blueberries)

Preparation Steps

- In a mixing bowl, blend the Greek yogurt with ground cinnamon, sugar-free sweetener, and vanilla extract until well combined.
- In four serving glasses or bowls, start layering the yogurt mixture.
- Add a layer of chopped almonds and unsweetened coconut flakes over the yogurt.
- Repeat the layers until all ingredients are used, finishing with a layer of nuts and coconut.
- Optionally, top each parfait with a few berries for added color and a hint of sweetness.
- Serve immediately for a fresh and flavorful keto-friendly breakfast.

🥣	**Preparation Time : 5 min**
🍳	**Cook Time : 0 min**
🕐	**Total Time: 5 min**
✗	**Serving : 4**

NUTRITIONAL INFO (per serving)

Calories: 280

Total Fat: 20g

Protein: 15g

Total Carbohydrates: 10g

Net Carbs: 7g

ALLERGEN
Contains Dairy (yogurt), Nuts , almond

EGG MUFFINS WITH SPINACH AND CHEESE

Egg Muffins with Spinach and Cheese are a delightful and convenient breakfast option for those on a ketogenic diet. Packed with protein, these muffins are easy to make, perfect for meal prep, and great for a quick, on-the-go breakfast. The combination of eggs, spinach, and cheese makes for a delicious and nutritious start to your day.

Ingredients

- 8 large eggs
- 1 cup fresh spinach, chopped
- 1/2 cup shredded cheddar cheese
- 1/4 cup milk (or almond milk for a lower carb option)
- Salt and pepper, to taste
- Cooking spray or butter for greasing muffin tin
- Optional: diced bell peppers or cooked bacon bits for added flavor

Preparation Steps

- Preheat your oven to 350°F (175°C). Grease a 12-cup muffin tin with cooking spray or butter.
- In a large bowl, whisk together the eggs, milk, salt, and pepper.
- Stir in the chopped spinach and shredded cheddar cheese. Add optional ingredients like bell peppers or bacon bits if desired.
- Pour the egg mixture evenly into the prepared muffin cups, filling each about two-thirds full.
- Bake in the preheated oven for 18-20 minutes, or until the egg muffins are set and lightly golden on top.
- Remove from oven and let cool for a few minutes before removing from the muffin tin.
- Serve the egg muffins warm.

Preparation Time : 10 min

Cook Time : 20 min

Total Time: 30 min

Serving : 4 (2 muffins per serving)

NUTRITIONAL INFO (per serving)

Calories: 220

Total Fat: 16g

Protein: 16g

Total Carbohydrates: 2g

Net Carbs: 2g

ALLERGEN
Contains Eggs, Dairy (cheese)

COTTAGE CHEESE BOWL

The Cottage Cheese Bowl is a simple, yet nutritious and satisfying breakfast option for those following a ketogenic diet. Combining the creamy texture of cottage cheese with a variety of toppings, this bowl is high in protein and customizable to your taste preferences. It's an excellent choice for a quick and easy breakfast that keeps you full and energized.

Ingredients

- 2 cups full-fat cottage cheese
- 1/2 cup almonds, chopped
- 1/4 cup flaxseeds, ground
- Optional toppings: cinnamon, a few berries (like raspberries or blueberries), or a drizzle of sugar-free syrup

Preparation Steps

- Divide the cottage cheese evenly among four bowls.
- Sprinkle each bowl with an equal amount of chopped almonds and ground flaxseeds.
- Add any optional toppings like a sprinkle of cinnamon, a handful of berries, or a drizzle of sugar-free syrup for added flavor.
- Serve immediately, enjoying the mix of textures and flavors in each bite.

🥣	**Preparation Time : 5 min**
🥄	**Cook Time : 0 min**
🕐	**Total Time: 5 min**
🍴	**Serving : 4**

NUTRITIONAL INFO (per serving)

Calories: 250

Total Fat: 15g

Protein: 20g

Total Carbohydrates: 8g

Net Carbs: 5g

ALLERGEN
Contains Dairy (cottage cheese)

20
KETO
Lunch
RECIPES

KETO COBB SALAD

The Keto Cobb Salad is a hearty and colorful dish, perfect for a satisfying lunch. This classic salad is reimagined to fit a ketogenic lifestyle, featuring a variety of fresh ingredients and rich flavors, all while maintaining low carb content. It's a great way to enjoy a variety of textures and tastes in one meal.

Ingredients

- 4 cups mixed salad greens (like romaine, spinach, and arugula)
- 2 ripe avocados, diced
- 4 hard-boiled eggs, sliced
- 1 cup cherry tomatoes, halved
- 1 cup cooked chicken breast, diced
- 8 slices of bacon, cooked and crumbled
- 1/2 cup blue cheese, crumbled
- Optional dressing: olive oil and vinegar or keto-friendly ranch dressing

Preparation Steps

- Begin by preparing your ingredients: cook the bacon until crispy and chop it into small pieces, boil the eggs and slice them, and dice the cooked chicken breast.
- Wash and dry the mixed salad greens and arrange them as a base in a large serving bowl or on individual plates.
- Neatly arrange the diced avocados, sliced hard-boiled eggs, halved cherry tomatoes, diced chicken, crumbled bacon, and blue cheese over the greens. You can create rows of each ingredient for a visually appealing presentation.
- Serve the salad with a dressing of your choice on the side, such as a simple mix of olive oil and vinegar or a keto-friendly ranch dressing.
- Toss everything together just before eating for the best mix of flavors and textures.

🥣	**Preparation Time : 15 min**
🍳	**Cook Time : 10 min** (for cooking bacon and eggs)
🕐	**Total Time: 25 min**
🍴	**Serving : 4**

NUTRITIONAL INFO (per serving)

Calories: 450

Total Fat: 35g

Protein: 30g

Total Carbohydrates: 10g

Net Carbs: 6g

ALLERGEN
Contains Eggs, Dairy (cheese

GRILLED CHICKEN CAESAR SALAD

Grilled Chicken Caesar Salad is a classic dish reimagined for a ketogenic diet. Featuring succulent grilled chicken on a bed of crisp romaine lettuce, dressed with a rich, creamy Caesar dressing and topped with Parmesan shavings, it's a perfect combination of flavors and textures. This salad is not only delicious but also provides a healthy, low-carb meal that's easy to prepare.

Ingredients

- 4 boneless, skinless chicken breasts
- 2 tablespoons olive oil
- Salt and pepper, to taste
- 8 cups romaine lettuce, chopped
- 1/2 cup Caesar dressing, keto-friendly
- 1/2 cup Parmesan cheese, shaved or grated
- Lemon wedges, for serving
- Optional: a sprinkle of garlic powder for the chicken

Preparation Steps

- Preheat your grill to medium-high heat.
- Brush the chicken breasts with olive oil and season them with salt, pepper, and optional garlic powder.
- Grill the chicken for about 5 minutes per side, or until it's thoroughly cooked and has nice grill marks.
- Let the chicken rest for a few minutes, then slice it into strips.
- In a large bowl, toss the chopped romaine lettuce with the keto-friendly Caesar dressing until well coated.
- Divide the dressed lettuce among four plates.
- Top each salad with sliced grilled chicken and a generous sprinkle of Parmesan cheese.
- Serve each salad with a lemon wedge on the side.

Preparation Time : 10 min

Cook Time : 10 min (for grilling chicken)

Total Time: 20 min

Serving : 4

NUTRITIONAL INFO (per serving)

Calories: 350

Total Fat: 22g

Protein: 30g

Total Carbohydrates: 6g

Net Carbs: 4g

ALLERGEN
Contains Dairy (Parmesan cheese)

ZUCCHINI NOODLE ALFREDO

Zucchini Noodle Alfredo is a delicious, low-carb twist on the classic Alfredo pasta. Using spiralized zucchini as a substitute for traditional noodles, this dish offers a lighter, keto-friendly version that's just as satisfying and flavorful. The creamy Alfredo sauce perfectly complements the tender zucchini noodles, making it an ideal choice for a comforting and healthy lunch.

Ingredients

- 4 medium zucchinis, spiralized into noodles
- 2 tablespoons unsalted butter
- 1 cup heavy cream
- 1 clove garlic, minced
- 1 cup grated Parmesan cheese
- Salt and pepper, to taste
- Optional: chopped parsley or basil for garnish

Preparation Steps

- Heat the butter in a large skillet over medium heat. Add the minced garlic and sauté for about 1 minute until fragrant.
- Pour in the heavy cream and bring it to a simmer. Let it cook for about 5 minutes, stirring occasionally, until it begins to thicken.
- Add the grated Parmesan cheese to the skillet, stirring until the cheese melts into the cream and the sauce becomes creamy. Season with salt and pepper to taste.
- Add the spiralized zucchini noodles to the skillet with the Alfredo sauce. Toss gently to coat the noodles in the sauce and cook for 2-3 minutes until the noodles are tender but still firm.
- Once the noodles are cooked to your liking, remove the skillet from heat.
- erve the Zucchini Noodle Alfredo hot, garnished with chopped parsley or basil if desired.

	Preparation Time : 15 min
	Cook Time : 10 min
	Total Time: 25 min
	Serving : 4

NUTRITIONAL INFO (per serving)

Calories: 390

Total Fat: 35g

Protein: 13g

Total Carbohydrates: 8g

Net Carbs: 6g

ALLERGEN
Contains Dairy (heavy cream, cheese)

TUNA SALAD STUFFED AVOCADOS

Tuna Salad Stuffed Avocados are a fresh and nutritious lunch option, perfect for a ketogenic diet. This dish combines the rich flavors of tuna salad with the creamy texture of avocado, creating a satisfying and healthy meal. It's an excellent way to enjoy a high-protein, low-carb dish that's both easy to prepare and delicious.

Ingredients

- 2 large avocados, halved and pitted
- 1 can (5 ounces) tuna in water, drained
- 1/4 cup mayonnaise, preferably sugar-free
- 2 tablespoons red onion, finely chopped
- 1 celery stalk, finely chopped
- 1 tablespoon lemon juice
- Salt and pepper to taste
- Optional: chopped fresh herbs like dill or parsley

Preparation Steps

- In a mixing bowl, combine the drained tuna, mayonnaise, chopped red onion, chopped celery, and lemon juice. Mix well until all the ingredients are evenly incorporated.
- Season the tuna salad with salt and pepper to taste. Add the optional chopped herbs if desired.
- Carefully scoop out some of the flesh from each avocado half to create a larger cavity for the salad. You can chop the removed avocado and mix it into the tuna salad if you like.
- Spoon the tuna salad mixture into the cavities of the avocado halves, distributing it evenly among them.
- Serve the stuffed avocados immediately, or refrigerate until ready to eat.

Preparation Time : 10 min

Cook Time : 0 min

Total Time: 10 min

Serving : 4

NUTRITIONAL INFO (per serving)

Calories: 300

Total Fat: 25g

Protein: 15g

Total Carbohydrates: 9g

Net Carbs: 3g

ALLERGEN
Contains Fish (tuna)

KETO BLT WRAP

The Keto BLT Wrap takes the classic flavors of a BLT sandwich and presents them in a low-carb, keto-friendly format. Using lettuce as the wrap, this dish combines crispy bacon, juicy tomatoes, and fresh lettuce, offering a delicious and satisfying lunch option that's both simple and aligned with ketogenic dietary goals.

Ingredients

- 8 large lettuce leaves (Romaine or iceberg work well)
- 8 slices of bacon, cooked until crispy
- 1 large tomato, sliced
- 4 tablespoons mayonnaise, preferably sugar-free
- Salt and pepper, to taste
- Optional: avocado slices or a sprinkle of garlic powder for extra flavor

Preparation Steps

- Cook the bacon in a skillet over medium heat until crispy. Drain on paper towels and set aside.
- Wash and dry the lettuce leaves. If using Romaine lettuce, trim the hard stem for easier wrapping.
- Lay out the lettuce leaves on a flat surface. Spread about 1/2 tablespoon of mayonnaise on each leaf.
- Place two slices of bacon on each lettuce leaf. Add a couple of tomato slices on top of the bacon. Season with salt and pepper, and add avocado slices if using.
- Carefully roll the lettuce leaves around the fillings, tucking in the edges to form a wrap.
- Serve the Keto BLT Wraps immediately, or wrap them in parchment paper for an on-the-go lunch.

Preparation Time : 10 min

Cook Time : 10 min (for cooking bacon)

Total Time: 20 min

Serving : 4

NUTRITIONAL INFO (per serving)

Calories: 230

Total Fat: 20g

Protein: 10g

Total Carbohydrates: 4g

Net Carbs: 2g

ALLERGEN
Contains Pork (bacon)

BROCCOLI AND CHEESE SOUP

Broccoli and Cheese Soup is a classic comfort food, reimagined here to fit a ketogenic diet. This rich and creamy soup combines the earthy taste of broccoli with the sharpness of cheese, creating a hearty and satisfying meal that's perfect for a keto-friendly lunch.

Ingredients

- 4 cups broccoli florets, chopped
- 1 small onion, diced
- 2 cloves garlic, minced
- 2 cups chicken or vegetable broth
- 1 cup heavy cream
- 1 1/2 cups shredded cheddar cheese
- 2 tablespoons butter
- Salt and pepper, to taste
- Optional: a pinch of nutmeg

Preparation Steps

- In a large pot, melt the butter over medium heat. Add the diced onion and minced garlic, sautéing until the onion is translucent, about 3-4 minutes.
- Add the broccoli florets to the pot and sauté for another 2-3 minutes.
- Pour in the chicken or vegetable broth and bring the mixture to a boil. Reduce the heat and let it simmer until the broccoli is tender, about 10 minutes.
- Using an immersion blender (or transferring to a regular blender in batches), purée the soup until it reaches your desired consistency.
- Return the soup to the pot (if using a regular blender) and stir in the heavy cream. Heat through without bringing to a boil.
- Gradually add the shredded cheddar cheese, stirring constantly until the cheese is fully melted and the soup is creamy. Season with salt, pepper, and a pinch of nutmeg if desired.
- Serve the soup hot, dividing it evenly among four bowls.

	Preparation Time : 10 min
	Cook Time : 20 min
	Total Time: 30 min
	Serving : 4

NUTRITIONAL INFO (per serving)

Calories: 350

Total Fat: 30g

Protein: 15g

Total Carbohydrates: 8g

Net Carbs: 5g

ALLERGEN
Contains Dairy (cheese, butter or cream)

KETO TURKEY AND CHEESE ROLL-UPS

Keto Turkey and Cheese Roll-Ups are a simple, delicious, and convenient lunch option for those on a ketogenic diet. Combining lean turkey slices with creamy cheese, these roll-ups are perfect for a quick and satisfying meal that's low in carbs but high in flavor. They're ideal for a light lunch or a snack and are very easy to prepare.

Ingredients

- 8 slices of deli turkey breast (preferably low in sodium and without added sugars)
- 4 slices of cheddar or Swiss cheese
- 1/4 cup mayonnaise, preferably sugar-free
- 1/4 cup mustard or sugar-free relish (optional)
- Optional fillings: lettuce leaves, thinly sliced cucumbers, or avocado slices

Preparation Steps

- Lay out the turkey slices on a flat surface. If the slices are very thin, you may want to stack two together for each roll-up.
- Spread a thin layer of mayonnaise (and mustard or relish, if using) on each turkey slice.
- Place a slice of cheese on each turkey slice. Add optional fillings like lettuce, cucumber, or avocado on top of the cheese.
- Carefully roll up the turkey slices tightly around the cheese and fillings.
- Cut each roll-up in half, if desired, for easier eating.
- Serve the turkey and cheese roll-ups immediately, or refrigerate until ready to eat.

	Preparation Time : 5 min
	Cook Time : 0 min
	Total Time: 5 min
	Serving : 4

NUTRITIONAL INFO (per serving)

Calories: 200

Total Fat: 15g

Protein: 15g

Total Carbohydrates: 1g

Net Carbs: 1g

ALLERGEN
Contains Dairy (cheese), Poultry (turkey)

STUFFED BELL PEPPERS

Stuffed Bell Peppers are a flavorful and nutritious meal that fits beautifully into a ketogenic diet. These peppers are filled with a savory mixture of ground meat, cheese, and spices, then baked until tender. They offer a perfect combination of protein, healthy fats, and vegetables, making them a satisfying and balanced keto-friendly lunch option.

Ingredients

- 4 bell peppers, any color, tops cut off and seeds removed
- 1 pound ground beef or turkey
- 1/2 cup onion, finely chopped
- 2 cloves garlic, minced
- 1 cup cauliflower rice
- 1 cup shredded cheddar cheese
- 1 teaspoon paprika
- Salt and pepper, to taste
- 2 tablespoons olive oil
- Optional: 1/4 cup low-carb tomato sauce

Preparation Steps

- Preheat your oven to 350°F (175°C).
- In a skillet, heat the olive oil over medium heat. Add the onions and garlic, sautéing until fragrant and translucent.
- Add the ground beef or turkey to the skillet. Cook until browned, breaking it up with a spoon as it cooks.
- Stir in the cauliflower rice, paprika, salt, and pepper. Cook for an additional 5 minutes. Remove from heat.
- If using, stir in the low-carb tomato sauce to the meat mixture.
- Spoon the mixture into the hollowed-out bell peppers, packing it in tightly. Place the stuffed peppers in a baking dish.
- Bake in the preheated oven for 20-25 minutes, or until the peppers are tender.
- Sprinkle the shredded cheddar cheese over the tops of the peppers and return to the oven. Bake for an additional 5 minutes, or until the cheese is melted and bubbly.
- Serve the stuffed bell peppers hot, garnished with additional herbs or spices if desired.

🥣	**Preparation Time : 15 min**
🥄	**Cook Time : 30 min**
🕐	**Total Time: 45 min**
🍴	**Serving : 4**

NUTRITIONAL INFO (per serving)

Calories: 400

Total Fat: 28g

Protein: 25g

Total Carbohydrates: 12g

Net Carbs: 9g

ALLERGEN

Contains Dairy (cheese), depending on the meat and other fillings used

EGG SALAD LETTUCE WRAPS

Egg Salad Lettuce Wraps offer a refreshing and light take on traditional egg salad. By using crisp lettuce leaves as the wrap, this dish becomes a perfect, carb-conscious alternative that aligns with a ketogenic diet. It's a simple yet delightful way to enjoy a classic egg salad with a healthy twist, ideal for a satisfying and easy-to-prepare lunch.

Ingredients

- 6 large eggs, hard-boiled and peeled
- 1/4 cup mayonnaise, preferably sugar-free
- 2 tablespoons Dijon mustard
- 1/4 cup celery, finely chopped
- Salt and pepper to taste
- 8 large lettuce leaves (such as Bibb or Romaine)
- Optional: paprika or chopped chives for garnish

Preparation Steps

- In a bowl, roughly chop the hard-boiled eggs.
- Add the mayonnaise, Dijon mustard, and chopped celery to the eggs. Gently mix until all ingredients are well combined. Season the egg salad with salt and pepper to taste.
- Lay out the lettuce leaves on a flat surface. Spoon an equal amount of the egg salad into the center of each lettuce leaf.
- Carefully fold the lettuce around the egg salad, tucking in the edges to form a wrap.
- If desired, sprinkle the wraps with paprika or chopped chives for extra flavor and a decorative touch.
- Serve the egg salad lettuce wraps immediately, or chill in the refrigerator for a cool and refreshing lunch option.

	Preparation Time : 15 min
	Cook Time : 0 min
🕐	**Total Time: 15 min**
✕	**Serving : 4**

NUTRITIONAL INFO (per serving)

Calories: 220

Total Fat: 18g

Protein: 12g

Total Carbohydrates: 2g

Net Carbs: 1g

ALLERGEN
Contains Eggs

CAULIFLOWER RICE STIR-FRY

Cauliflower Rice Stir-Fry is a vibrant and flavorful dish that serves as an excellent low-carb alternative to traditional stir-fried rice. Packed with vegetables and your choice of protein, this meal is not only nutritious and fulfilling but also aligns perfectly with a ketogenic diet. It's a versatile and easy-to-make dish that can be customized to your taste preferences.

Ingredients

- 1 large head of cauliflower, grated or processed into 'rice'
- 2 tablespoons coconut oil or olive oil
- 1 medium onion, diced
- 2 cloves garlic, minced
- 1 cup mixed bell peppers, sliced
- 1/2 cup carrots, julienned
- 1/2 cup peas (optional, if within carb limits)
- 2 eggs, lightly beaten
- 1/2 cup cooked chicken, shrimp, or tofu, diced (optional)
- 2 tablespoons soy sauce or tamari (gluten-free)
- Salt and pepper, to taste

Preparation Steps

- Prepare the cauliflower rice by grating the cauliflower or pulsing it in a food processor until it resembles rice grains.
- Heat a large skillet or wok over medium heat. Add 1 tablespoon of oil, then sauté the onion and garlic until fragrant.
- Add the mixed bell peppers and carrots to the skillet. Stir-fry until the vegetables are tender-crisp.
- Move the vegetables to one side of the skillet. Add the remaining oil and pour in the beaten eggs. Scramble the eggs until cooked through.
- Add the cauliflower rice, cooked protein (if using), and peas to the skillet. Drizzle with soy sauce or tamari and mix everything together. Stir-fry for another 5-7 minutes until the cauliflower rice is tender.
- Season with salt and pepper to taste. Garnish with green onions, sesame seeds, or a drizzle of sesame oil if desired.
- Serve the cauliflower rice stir-fry hot, divided into four portions.

🍚	**Preparation Time : 15 min**
🥄	**Cook Time : 15 min**
🕐	**Total Time: 30 min**
🍴	**Serving : 4**

NUTRITIONAL INFO (per serving)

Calories: 180

Total Fat: 10g

Protein: 8g

Total Carbohydrates: 15g

Net Carbs: 10g

ALLERGEN

Contains Eggs, Soy (soy sauce), Nuts (if using nut-based oils or ingredients)

SHRIMP AVOCADO SALAD

Shrimp Avocado Salad is a refreshing and light dish, ideal for a ketogenic lunch. This salad combines succulent shrimp with creamy avocado and crisp vegetables, dressed in a tangy vinaigrette. It's a perfect blend of protein, healthy fats, and flavor, making it a satisfying yet easy-to-prepare meal.

Ingredients

- 1 pound shrimp, peeled and deveined
- 2 ripe avocados, diced
- 1 cup cucumber, diced
- 1/2 cup cherry tomatoes, halved
- 1/4 cup red onion, thinly sliced
- 1/4 cup fresh cilantro, chopped
- 2 tablespoons olive oil
- Juice of 1 lime
- Salt and pepper, to taste
- Optional: 1 clove garlic, minced, and a pinch of chili flakes for extra flavor

Preparation Steps

- Heat a skillet over medium-high heat. Add 1 tablespoon of olive oil and the shrimp. Cook the shrimp for 2-3 minutes on each side, or until they are pink and opaque. Season with salt and pepper. Set aside to cool.
- In a large bowl, combine the diced avocados, cucumber, cherry tomatoes, red onion, and cilantro.
- In a small bowl, whisk together the remaining olive oil, lime juice, minced garlic (if using), and chili flakes (if using) to make the dressing.
- Pour the dressing over the salad and gently toss to coat all the ingredients.
- Add the cooked shrimp to the salad and toss lightly to combine.
- Season with additional salt and pepper if needed.
- Serve the shrimp avocado salad immediately, or chill in the refrigerator for a refreshing and cool meal.

Preparation Time : 15 min

Cook Time : 5 min (for cooking shrimps)

Total Time: 20 min

Serving : 4

NUTRITIONAL INFO (per serving)

Calories: 300

Total Fat: 20g

Protein: 25g

Total Carbohydrates: 10g

Net Carbs: 6g

ALLERGEN
Contains Shellfish (shrimp)

KETO BEEF TACOS

Keto Beef Tacos are a fantastic way to enjoy the classic flavors of tacos without the carbs. Using lettuce leaves as taco shells, this dish is filled with savory ground beef and topped with fresh, flavorful ingredients. It's a fun and delicious meal that's perfect for a keto-friendly lunch or dinner.

Ingredients

- 8 large lettuce leaves (such as romaine or butter lettuce)
- 1 pound ground beef
- 1 tablespoon taco seasoning (sugar-free)
- 1/2 cup shredded cheddar cheese
- 1/4 cup diced tomatoes
- 1/4 cup diced red onion
- 1/4 cup sour cream
- 1 avocado, diced
- Optional: fresh cilantro, lime wedges, and sliced jalapeños for garnish

Preparation Steps

- In a skillet over medium heat, cook the ground beef until browned, breaking it up with a spoon as it cooks.
- Drain excess fat and stir in the taco seasoning. Cook for an additional 2-3 minutes.
- Prepare the lettuce leaves by washing and drying them thoroughly.
- Assemble the tacos by dividing the cooked beef among the lettuce leaves.
- Top each taco with shredded cheese, diced tomatoes, red onion, and avocado.
- Add a dollop of sour cream to each taco.
- Garnish with optional cilantro, lime wedges, and sliced jalapeños if desired.
- Serve the keto beef tacos immediately.

🥣	**Preparation Time : 10 min**
🥄	**Cook Time : 15 min**
🕐	**Total Time: 25 min**
🍴	**Serving : 4 (2 tacos per serving)**

NUTRITIONAL INFO (per serving)

Calories: 400

Total Fat: 28g

Protein: 25g

Total Carbohydrates: 8g

Net Carbs: 5g

ALLERGEN

Contains dairy (cheddar cheese, sour cream). Can be modified to exclude dairy if needed.

CHICKEN AVOCADO CAPRESE SALAD

Chicken Avocado Caprese Salad is a fresh and delightful twist on the traditional Caprese salad. This dish combines succulent grilled chicken with creamy avocado, fresh mozzarella, and ripe tomatoes, all drizzled with a balsamic reduction. It's a perfect blend of protein, healthy fats, and vibrant flavors, making it an ideal choice for a light yet satisfying keto-friendly lunch.

Ingredients

- 2 boneless, skinless chicken breasts
- 2 avocados, sliced
- 8 oz fresh mozzarella cheese, sliced
- 2 large tomatoes, sliced
- 1/4 cup fresh basil leaves
- 2 tablespoons olive oil
- Salt and pepper, to taste
- Balsamic glaze for drizzling

Preparation Steps

- Preheat a grill or grill pan over medium-high heat.
- Brush the chicken breasts with 1 tablespoon of olive oil and season with salt and pepper.
- Grill the chicken for 5-6 minutes on each side, or until fully cooked and juicy. Let it rest for a few minutes, then slice it.
- Arrange the sliced tomatoes, fresh mozzarella, and avocado on a serving platter or individual plates.
- Add the grilled chicken slices to the salad.
- Scatter the fresh basil leaves over the top.
- Drizzle the remaining olive oil and balsamic glaze over the salad.
- Season with additional salt and pepper to taste.
- Serve the Chicken Avocado Caprese Salad immediately, enjoying the harmony of flavors and textures.

	Preparation Time : 15 min
	Cook Time : 10 min
	Total Time: 25 min
	Serving : 4

NUTRITIONAL INFO (per serving)

Calories: 400

Total Fat: 28g

Protein: 25g

Total Carbohydrates: 12g

Net Carbs: 9g

ALLERGEN
Contains dairy (mozzarella cheese).

SPINACH AND FETA STUFFED CHICKEN

Spinach and Feta Stuffed Chicken is a delicious and elegant dish, perfect for a ketogenic lunch or dinner. This recipe involves stuffing tender chicken breasts with a flavorful mixture of spinach and feta cheese, creating a meal that is not only visually appealing but also packed with nutrients and taste. It's a great way to elevate a simple chicken dish into something special while keeping it low-carb and keto-friendly.

Ingredients

- 4 boneless, skinless chicken breasts
- 2 cups fresh spinach, chopped
- 1/2 cup feta cheese, crumbled
- 2 cloves garlic, minced
- 2 tablespoons olive oil
- Salt and pepper, to taste
- Optional: lemon wedges for serving

Preparation Steps

- Preheat your oven to 375°F (190°C).
- In a skillet, heat 1 tablespoon of olive oil over medium heat. Add the garlic and spinach, cooking until the spinach is wilted. Remove from heat and let it cool slightly.
- Stir the crumbled feta cheese into the spinach mixture.
- Make a horizontal cut in each chicken breast to create a pocket. Be careful not to cut all the way through.
- Stuff each chicken breast with an equal amount of the spinach and feta mixture. Secure the openings with toothpicks if necessary.
- Season the outside of the chicken breasts with salt and pepper.
- In the same skillet, heat the remaining olive oil over medium-high heat. Sear the chicken on both sides until golden brown.
- Transfer the skillet to the preheated oven and bake for 20 minutes, or until the chicken is cooked through and the juices run clear.
- Serve the Spinach and Feta Stuffed Chicken warm, with optional lemon wedges on the side.

Preparation Time : 15 min	
Cook Time : 25 min	
Total Time: 40 min	
Serving : 4	

NUTRITIONAL INFO (per serving)

Calories: 300

Total Fat: 15g

Protein: 35g

Total Carbohydrates: 2g

Net Carbs: 1g

ALLERGEN
Contains dairy (feta cheese).

KETO MEATLOAF

Keto Meatloaf is a hearty and comforting meal that's perfect for a low-carb diet. This version of the classic meatloaf is made without breadcrumbs, relying instead on keto-friendly ingredients to bind the meat together while keeping the flavors rich and satisfying. It's an ideal dish for a fulfilling lunch or dinner, providing all the comfort of traditional meatloaf without the carbs.

Ingredients

- 1 1/2 pounds ground beef (or a mix of ground beef and pork)
- 1/2 cup almond flour
- 1 egg
- 1/2 cup grated Parmesan cheese
- 1 small onion, finely chopped
- 2 cloves garlic, minced
- 2 tablespoons Worcestershire sauce
- 1 tablespoon tomato paste
- Salt and pepper, to taste
- Optional: 1/2 cup low-carb ketchup or tomato sauce for topping

Preparation Steps

- Preheat your oven to 350°F (175°C).
- In a large bowl, combine the ground beef, almond flour, egg, grated Parmesan, chopped onion, minced garlic, Worcestershire sauce, and tomato paste. Season with salt and pepper.
- Mix the ingredients together until well combined. Avoid overmixing to keep the meatloaf tender.
- Shape the mixture into a loaf and place it in a loaf pan or on a baking sheet lined with parchment paper.
- If using, spread the low-carb ketchup or tomato sauce over the top of the meatloaf.
- Bake in the preheated oven for about 50 minutes, or until the meatloaf is cooked through and has an internal temperature of 160°F (71°C).
- Remove from the oven and let it rest for 10 minutes before slicing.
- Serve the Keto Meatloaf warm, with your choice of keto-friendly sides.

 Preparation Time : 15 min

 Cook Time : 50 min

Total Time: 1 hour 5 min

Serving : 4

NUTRITIONAL INFO (per serving)

Calories: 400

Total Fat: 25g

Protein: 35g

Total Carbohydrates: 5g

Net Carbs: 3g

ALLERGEN
Contains nuts (almond flour) and dairy (Parmesan cheese).

SALMON AND ASPARAGUS FOIL PACKS

Salmon and Asparagus Foil Packs are a simple, healthy, and delicious meal perfect for a ketogenic diet. This cooking method locks in flavor and moisture, resulting in tender, perfectly cooked salmon and asparagus. It's an excellent choice for a nutritious lunch or dinner, with minimal cleanup required.

Ingredients

- 4 salmon fillets (about 6 ounces each)
- 1 bunch asparagus, trimmed
- 2 tablespoons olive oil
- 1 lemon, thinly sliced
- Salt and pepper, to taste
- Optional: garlic powder, dill, or other herbs for added flavor

Preparation Steps

- Preheat your oven to 400°F (200°C) or prepare your grill for medium heat.
- Cut four sheets of aluminum foil, each large enough to wrap a salmon fillet and a portion of asparagus.
- Place a salmon fillet and a quarter of the asparagus on each foil sheet.
- Drizzle each with olive oil and season with salt, pepper, and optional herbs or garlic powder.
- Top each salmon fillet with a few lemon slices.
- Fold the foil over the salmon and asparagus, sealing the edges to form a packet.
- Place the foil packets on a baking sheet and bake in the preheated oven for 20 minutes, or grill over medium heat for 15-20 minutes, until the salmon is cooked through and the asparagus is tender.
- Carefully open the foil packets (watch out for steam) and serve immediately.

Preparation Time : 10 min

Cook Time : 20 min

Total Time: 30 min

Serving : 4

NUTRITIONAL INFO (per serving)

Calories: 350

Total Fat: 22g

Protein: 34g

Total Carbohydrates: 4g

Net Carbs: 2g

ALLERGEN
Fish (salmon).

CREAMY MUSHROOM CHICKEN

Creamy Mushroom Chicken is a sumptuous and satisfying dish that perfectly fits a ketogenic lifestyle. This recipe features tender chicken breasts cooked in a rich and creamy mushroom sauce, offering a luxurious and comforting meal that's simple to prepare yet feels indulgent. It's ideal for a keto-friendly lunch or dinner that's both hearty and flavorful.

Ingredients

- 4 boneless, skinless chicken breasts
- 2 tablespoons olive oil
- Salt and pepper, to taste
- 1 cup mushrooms, sliced
- 2 cloves garlic, minced
- 1 cup heavy cream
- 1/2 cup chicken broth
- 1/4 cup grated Parmesan cheese
- Optional: fresh thyme or parsley for garnish

Preparation Steps

- Season the chicken breasts with salt and pepper.
- Heat olive oil in a large skillet over medium heat. Add the chicken breasts and cook for 5-7 minutes on each side, or until golden brown and cooked through. Remove from the skillet and set aside.
- In the same skillet, add the sliced mushrooms and minced garlic. Sauté for a few minutes until the mushrooms are soft and browned.
- Pour in the heavy cream and chicken broth, stirring to combine. Bring to a simmer.
- Add the grated Parmesan cheese to the skillet, stirring until the sauce thickens.
- Return the cooked chicken breasts to the skillet, spooning the sauce over them. Cook for an additional 5 minutes, allowing the chicken to absorb the flavors of the sauce.
- Garnish with fresh thyme or parsley, if desired.
- Serve the Creamy Mushroom Chicken hot

 Preparation Time : 10 min

 Cook Time : 25 min

Total Time: 35 min

Serving : 4

NUTRITIONAL INFO (per serving)

Calories: 420

Total Fat: 30g

Protein: 32g

Total Carbohydrates: 4g

Net Carbs: 3g

ALLERGEN
Contains dairy (heavy cream, Parmesan cheese).

KETO GREEK SALAD

Keto Greek Salad is a refreshing and flavorful dish, perfect for a light and healthy ketogenic meal. This salad combines crisp cucumbers, juicy tomatoes, tangy olives, and creamy feta cheese, all tossed in a zesty Greek dressing. It's a simple yet delicious way to enjoy a classic salad that's both low in carbs and high in taste.

Ingredients

- 2 medium cucumbers, diced
- 2 large tomatoes, diced
- 1/2 red onion, thinly sliced
- 1 cup Kalamata olives, pitted and halved
- 1 cup feta cheese, crumbled
- 1/4 cup olive oil
- 2 tablespoons red wine vinegar
- 1 teaspoon dried oregano
- Salt and pepper, to taste
- Optional: 1 tablespoon fresh lemon juice for added zest

Preparation Steps

- In a large salad bowl, combine the diced cucumbers, tomatoes, sliced red onion, Kalamata olives, and crumbled feta cheese.
- In a small bowl, whisk together the olive oil, red wine vinegar, dried oregano, and optional lemon juice. Season with salt and pepper to taste.
- Pour the dressing over the salad and toss gently to coat all the ingredients evenly.
- Let the salad sit for a few minutes to allow the flavors to meld together.
- Serve the Keto Greek Salad chilled or at room temperature.

🥣	**Preparation Time : 10 min**
🥘	**Cook Time : 0 min**
🕐	**Total Time: 10 min**
🍴	**Serving : 4**

NUTRITIONAL INFO (per serving)

Calories: 250

Total Fat: 22g

Protein: 6g

Total Carbohydrates: 10g

Net Carbs: 7g

ALLERGEN
Contains dairy (feta cheese).

BACON-WRAPPED ASPARAGUS

Bacon-Wrapped Asparagus is a delicious and elegant dish, perfect for those on a ketogenic diet. This recipe combines the savory flavor of bacon with the tender crunch of asparagus, creating a delightful contrast of textures. It's an easy-to-make appetizer or side dish that adds a touch of sophistication to any meal.

Ingredients

- 16 asparagus spears, ends trimmed
- 8 slices of bacon
- Salt and pepper, to taste
- Optional: a drizzle of olive oil or a sprinkle of Parmesan cheese for extra flavor

Preparation Steps

- Preheat your oven to 400°F (200°C). Line a baking sheet with parchment paper.
- Wrap each asparagus spear with half a slice of bacon, starting from the bottom and spiraling up to the tip. Place the wrapped spears on the prepared baking sheet.
- Optionally, lightly drizzle the asparagus with olive oil and season with salt and pepper. If using, sprinkle with Parmesan cheese.
- Bake in the preheated oven for 15-20 minutes, or until the bacon is crispy and the asparagus is tender.
- Serve the bacon-wrapped asparagus hot, either as an appetizer or a side dish.

Preparation Time : 10 min

Cook Time : 20 min

Total Time: 30 min

Serving : 4

NUTRITIONAL INFO (per serving)

Calories: 150

Total Fat: 12g

Protein: 10g

Total Carbohydrates: 3g

Net Carbs: 2g

ALLERGEN
Contains pork (bacon). Optional Parmesan cheese contains dairy.

KETO SHEPHERD'S PIE

Keto Shepherd's Pie is a comforting and hearty dish that adapts the classic recipe to fit a low-carb, ketogenic diet. Instead of the traditional potato topping, this version uses a flavorful cauliflower mash, making it just as satisfying but much more keto-friendly. Packed with savory ground meat and vegetables, it's a perfect meal for those looking for a comforting and nutritious keto option.

Ingredients

-For the Filling:
- 1 pound ground beef or lamb
- 1 small onion, diced
- 2 cloves garlic, minced
- 1 cup chopped carrots (optional, if within carb limits)
- 1 cup frozen peas (optional, if within carb limits)
- 1/2 cup beef broth
- 2 tablespoons tomato paste
- 1 teaspoon Worcestershire sauce
- Salt and pepper, to taste

-For the Cauliflower Mash:
- 1 large head cauliflower, cut into florets
- 2 tablespoons butter
- 1/4 cup heavy cream
- 1/2 cup grated cheddar cheese
- Salt and pepper, to taste

Preparation Steps

- Preheat the oven to 375°F (190°C).
- To make the cauliflower mash, boil the cauliflower florets in a large pot of water until very tender, about 10 minutes. Drain well and return to the pot.
- Add butter, heavy cream, salt, and pepper to the cauliflower. Mash until smooth and creamy. Stir in the cheddar cheese and set aside.
- For the filling, brown the ground beef or lamb in a large skillet over medium heat. Drain excess fat.
- Add the onion, garlic, and optional carrots to the meat and cook until softened.
- Stir in the frozen peas, beef broth, tomato paste, and Worcestershire sauce. Season with salt and pepper. Simmer the mixture for about 10 minutes, or until slightly thickened.
- Transfer the meat mixture to a baking dish.
- Spread the cauliflower mash evenly over the top of the meat.
- Bake in the preheated oven for 20-25 minutes, or until the top is golden and the edges are bubbly.
- Serve the Keto Shepherd's Pie hot.

🍲	**Preparation Time : 20 min**
🥄	**Cook Time : 30 min**
🕐	**Total Time: 50 min**
🍴	**Serving : 4**

NUTRITIONAL INFO (per serving)

Calories: 400

Total Fat: 28g

Protein: 25g

Total Carbohydrates: 12g

Net Carbs: 8g

ALLERGEN
Contains dairy (butter, heavy cream, cheddar cheese).

20
KETO
Dinner
RECIPES

LEMON BUTTER SALMON

Lemon Butter Salmon is a delicious and elegant dish that perfectly fits into a ketogenic diet. This recipe features succulent salmon fillets cooked in a rich and tangy lemon butter sauce, making it a flavorful and healthy option for any dinner. It's simple to prepare yet impressive enough for special occasions.

Ingredients

- 4 salmon fillets (about 6 ounces each)
- 4 tablespoons unsalted butter
- Juice and zest of 1 lemon
- 2 cloves garlic, minced
- Salt and pepper, to taste
- Optional: fresh dill or parsley for garnish

Preparation Steps

- Preheat your oven to 350°F (175°C).
- Season the salmon fillets with salt and pepper.
- In a skillet, melt the butter over medium heat. Add the minced garlic and cook for 1 minute until fragrant.
- Stir in the lemon juice and zest, then remove the skillet from heat.
- Place the salmon fillets in a baking dish. Pour the lemon butter sauce over the salmon.
- Bake in the preheated oven for 12-15 minutes, or until the salmon flakes easily with a fork.
- Garnish with fresh dill or parsley, if desired.
- Serve the Lemon Butter Salmon hot, spooning extra sauce from the baking dish over the fillets.

	Preparation Time : 10 min
	Cook Time : 15 min
	Total Time: 25 min
	Serving : 4

NUTRITIONAL INFO (per serving)

Calories: 300

Total Fat: 20g

Protein: 25g

Total Carbohydrates: 1g

Net Carbs: 1g

ALLERGEN
Contains fish (salmon) and dairy (butter).

KETO CHICKEN PARMESAN

Keto Chicken Parmesan is a delicious low-carb twist on the classic Italian dish. This version uses a mixture of almond flour and Parmesan cheese for the breading, achieving a crispy crust without the carbs. Topped with sugar-free marinara sauce and melted mozzarella, it's a comforting and satisfying meal that's perfect for anyone following a ketogenic diet.

Ingredients

- 4 boneless, skinless chicken breasts
- 1 cup almond flour
- 1/2 cup grated Parmesan cheese
- 1 teaspoon Italian seasoning
- 2 large eggs
- Salt and pepper, to taste
- 1/2 cup sugar-free marinara sauce
- 1 cup shredded mozzarella cheese
- 2 tablespoons olive oil
- Optional: fresh basil for garnish

Preparation Steps

- Preheat your oven to 375°F (190°C).
- In a shallow dish, mix together the almond flour, grated Parmesan cheese, and Italian seasoning. Season with salt and pepper.
- In another dish, beat the eggs.
- Dip each chicken breast first in the beaten eggs, then coat with the almond flour mixture, pressing to adhere.
- Heat olive oil in a large skillet over medium heat. Add the chicken and cook for 4-5 minutes on each side, or until golden brown.
- Transfer the chicken to a baking dish. Top each breast with an equal amount of marinara sauce, then sprinkle with shredded mozzarella cheese.
- Bake in the preheated oven for 15-20 minutes, or until the chicken is cooked through and the cheese is melted and bubbly.
- Garnish with fresh basil, if desired, before serving.

	Preparation Time : 15 min
	Cook Time : 25 min
	Total Time: 40 min
	Serving : 4

NUTRITIONAL INFO (per serving)

Calories: 450

Total Fat: 28g

Protein: 40g

Total Carbohydrates: 6g

Net Carbs: 4g

ALLERGEN
Contains nuts (almond flour), dairy (Parmesan and mozzarella cheese), and eggs.

KETO CHILI

Keto Chili is a hearty and robust dish perfect for those following a low-carb diet. This version of the classic chili foregoes beans in favor of a rich blend of ground meat, tomatoes, and a variety of spices. It's a comforting and filling meal that's packed with flavor, making it an ideal choice for a keto-friendly dinner.

Ingredients

- 1 pound ground beef (or a mix of beef and pork)
- 1 medium onion, diced
- 2 cloves garlic, minced
- 1 bell pepper, diced
- 1 can (14.5 ounces) diced tomatoes, with juice
- 2 tablespoons tomato paste
- 1 cup beef broth
- 1 tablespoon chili powder
- 1 teaspoon ground cumin
- 1 teaspoon paprika
- Salt and pepper, to taste
- Optional: diced jalapeños or red pepper flakes for added heat

Preparation Steps

- In a large pot or Dutch oven, cook the ground beef over medium heat until browned. Drain excess fat
- Add the diced onion, garlic, and bell pepper to the pot with the beef. Cook until the vegetables are softened, about 5 minutes.
- Stir in the diced tomatoes (with juice), tomato paste, and beef broth.
- Add the chili powder, cumin, paprika, salt, and pepper. If using, include diced jalapeños or red pepper flakes for extra heat.
- Bring the mixture to a boil, then reduce the heat to low and simmer, uncovered, for about 1 hour, stirring occasionally. The chili should thicken as it cooks.
- Taste and adjust seasonings as needed.
- Serve the chili hot, with optional keto-friendly toppings like shredded cheese, sour cream, or avocado.

Preparation Time : 15 min

Cook Time : 1 hour

Total Time: 1 hour 15 min

Serving : 4

NUTRITIONAL INFO (per serving)

Calories: 350

Total Fat: 22g

Protein: 25g

Total Carbohydrates: 10g

Net Carbs: 7g

ALLERGEN
No major allergens.

BACON-WRAPPED PORK TENDERLOIN

Bacon-Wrapped Pork Tenderloin is a succulent and flavorful dish that combines the tenderness of pork with the smoky richness of bacon. This dish not only presents a beautiful blend of flavors but also aligns perfectly with a ketogenic diet. It's an impressive meal that's surprisingly easy to prepare, making it perfect for a special dinner or a satisfying keto meal.

Ingredients

- 1 pork tenderloin (about 1 1/2 pounds)
- 8-10 slices of bacon
- Salt and pepper, to taste
- 1 teaspoon garlic powder
- 1 teaspoon smoked paprika
- Optional: fresh herbs (like rosemary or thyme) for seasoning

Preparation Steps

- Preheat your oven to 375°F (190°C).
- Season the pork tenderloin with salt, pepper, garlic powder, and smoked paprika. Optionally, add fresh herbs for additional flavor.
- Lay the bacon slices out on a work surface, slightly overlapping. Place the seasoned pork tenderloin on top of the bacon.
- Wrap the bacon slices around the pork tenderloin, securing them with toothpicks if necessary.
- Place the bacon-wrapped tenderloin on a baking sheet or in a roasting pan.
- Roast in the preheated oven for 25-30 minutes, or until the internal temperature of the pork reaches 145°F (63°C) and the bacon is crispy.
- Remove from the oven and let it rest for 5-10 minutes before slicing.
- Serve the Bacon-Wrapped Pork Tenderloin sliced, with your choice of keto-friendly sides.

🥣	**Preparation Time : 15 min**
🍳	**Cook Time : 30 min**
🕐	**Total Time: 45 min**
🍴	**Serving : 4**

NUTRITIONAL INFO (per serving)

Calories: 380

Total Fat: 22g

Protein: 38g

Total Carbohydrates: 1g

Net Carbs: 1g

ALLERGEN
No major allergens.

GARLIC BUTTER STEAK BITES

Garlic Butter Steak Bites are a quick and flavorful dish perfect for a ketogenic diet. These succulent bites of steak are cooked in a rich garlic butter sauce, offering a delicious combination of flavors. This dish is not only incredibly tasty but also easy to prepare, making it a great choice for a satisfying keto dinner.

Ingredients

- 1 1/2 pounds sirloin steak, cut into 1-inch cubes
- 4 tablespoons unsalted butter
- 3 cloves garlic, minced
- Salt and pepper, to taste
- Optional: chopped parsley or thyme for garnish

Preparation Steps

- Season the steak cubes generously with salt and pepper.
- Heat a large skillet over medium-high heat. Add the steak cubes in a single layer, working in batches if necessary, and sear them until browned on all sides, about 2-3 minutes per side.
- Remove the steak bites from the skillet and set them aside.
- In the same skillet, reduce the heat to medium and add the butter and minced garlic. Cook for 1-2 minutes, stirring frequently, until the garlic is fragrant but not browned.
- Return the steak bites to the skillet with the garlic butter. Stir to coat the steak bites in the sauce and cook for an additional 1-2 minutes.
- Garnish with chopped parsley or thyme, if desired.
- Serve the Garlic Butter Steak Bites hot, spooning any extra sauce over the top.

🥣	**Preparation Time : 10 min**
🥄	**Cook Time : 10 min**
🕐	**Total Time: 20 min**
✗	**Serving : 4**

NUTRITIONAL INFO (per serving)

Calories: 400

Total Fat: 28g

Protein: 35g

Total Carbohydrates: 1g

Net Carbs: 1g

ALLERGEN
Contains dairy (butter).

CAULIFLOWER FRIED RICE WITH CHICKEN

Cauliflower Fried Rice with Chicken is a delicious and healthy alternative to traditional fried rice, perfectly suited for a ketogenic diet. This dish features riced cauliflower stir-fried with chicken, vegetables, and savory seasonings, offering the same satisfying experience as regular fried rice but with significantly fewer carbs.

Ingredients

- 1 large head cauliflower, riced
- 2 boneless, skinless chicken breasts, cut into bite-sized pieces
- 3 tablespoons sesame oil or olive oil
- 2 eggs, lightly beaten
- 1 medium onion, diced
- 1 cup frozen peas and carrots (optional, if within carb limits)
- 2 cloves garlic, minced
- 1/4 cup soy sauce or tamari (gluten-free)
- Salt and pepper, to taste
- Optional: green onions and sesame seeds for garnish

Preparation Steps

- Rice the cauliflower by grating it or pulsing it in a food processor until it resembles rice grains. Set aside.
- In a large skillet or wok, heat 1 tablespoon of oil over medium-high heat. Add the chicken pieces, season with salt and pepper, and cook until browned and cooked through. Remove from the skillet and set aside.
- In the same skillet, add another tablespoon of oil and scramble the eggs. Once cooked, remove them from the skillet and set aside.
- Heat the remaining oil in the skillet. Add the diced onion and cook until translucent. Add the garlic and sauté for another minute.
- Increase the heat to high and add the riced cauliflower, stirring to combine with the onions and garlic. Cook for about 5-7 minutes, or until the cauliflower is tender.
- Add the peas and carrots, cooked chicken, and scrambled eggs back to the skillet. Pour in the soy sauce and stir everything together, cooking for another 2-3 minutes.
- Season with additional salt and pepper to taste.
- Garnish with green onions and sesame seeds, if desired, before serving.

🥣	**Preparation Time : 15 min**
🥄	**Cook Time : 20 min**
🕐	**Total Time: 35 min**
🍴	**Serving : 4**

NUTRITIONAL INFO (per serving)

Calories: 350

Total Fat: 18g

Protein: 25g

Total Carbohydrates: 15g

Net Carbs: 10g

ALLERGEN
Contains eggs and soy (soy sauce)

KETO SHRIMP AND BROCCOLI STIR-FRY

Keto Shrimp and Broccoli Stir-Fry is a quick, flavorful, and nutritious dinner option perfect for a ketogenic diet. This dish combines succulent shrimp and tender broccoli in a savory, garlic-infused sauce, delivering a satisfying meal that's both low in carbs and high in protein. It's an ideal choice for a wholesome and delicious keto-friendly dinner.

Ingredients

- 1 pound shrimp, peeled and deveined
- 2 cups broccoli florets
- 3 tablespoons olive oil
- 2 cloves garlic, minced
- 1 tablespoon soy sauce (or tamari for gluten-free)
- 1 teaspoon sesame oil
- 1/2 teaspoon ginger, grated
- Salt and pepper, to taste
- Optional: Red pepper flakes for a spicy kick
- Optional garnish: Sesame seeds and sliced green onions

Preparation Steps

- Heat 2 tablespoons of olive oil in a large skillet or wok over medium-high heat.
- Add the broccoli florets to the skillet and sauté for about 4-5 minutes, until they become tender but still have some crunch.
- Remove the broccoli from the skillet and set it aside.
- In the same skillet, add the remaining 1 tablespoon of olive oil and minced garlic. Sauté for 1 minute until fragrant.
- Add the shrimp to the skillet and season with salt and pepper. Cook for 2-3 minutes per side, or until the shrimp turn pink and opaque.
- In a small bowl, mix together the soy sauce (or tamari), sesame oil, and grated ginger. Pour this mixture over the shrimp in the skillet.
- Return the cooked broccoli to the skillet and toss everything together to combine and coat with the sauce. Cook for an additional 1-2 minutes.
- Optional: Add red pepper flakes for some heat, if desired.
- Serve the Keto Shrimp and Broccoli Stir-Fry hot, garnished with sesame seeds and sliced green onions, if desired.

🥣	**Preparation Time : 10 min**
🍳	**Cook Time : 15 min**
🕐	**Total Time: 25 min**
🍴	**Serving : 4**

NUTRITIONAL INFO (per serving)

Calories: 250

Total Fat: 15g

Protein: 24g

Total Carbohydrates: 6g

Net Carbs: 4g

ALLERGEN
Contains shellfish (shrimp), soy (soy sauce)

KETO EGGPLANT PARMESAN

Keto Eggplant Parmesan is a delightful low-carb version of the classic Italian dish. This recipe swaps traditional breaded coating with a keto-friendly alternative, offering the same delicious flavors and textures without the extra carbs. It's a comforting and satisfying meal that's perfect for anyone following a ketogenic lifestyle.

Ingredients

- 2 medium eggplants, sliced into 1/2 inch rounds
- Salt, to draw out moisture from eggplant
- 2 cups almond flour
- 2 large eggs, beaten
- 2 cups marinara sauce, sugar-free
- 2 cups shredded mozzarella cheese
- 1/2 cup grated Parmesan cheese
- 1 teaspoon Italian seasoning
- 2 tablespoons olive oil
- Optional: fresh basil leaves for garnish

Preparation Steps

- Preheat your oven to 375°F (190°C).
- Sprinkle salt on both sides of the eggplant slices and set aside for 10-15 minutes to draw out moisture. Pat dry with paper towels.
- Dip each eggplant slice into beaten eggs, then dredge in almond flour, coating evenly.
- Heat olive oil in a skillet over medium heat. Cook the eggplant slices in batches until golden brown on both sides. Transfer to a paper towel-lined plate.
- In a baking dish, spread a thin layer of marinara sauce. Layer the eggplant slices over the sauce.
- Top with a layer of mozzarella and Parmesan cheeses, then another layer of marinara sauce. Repeat the layers until all ingredients are used, ending with cheese on top.
- Sprinkle Italian seasoning over the cheese.
- Bake in the preheated oven for 25-30 minutes, or until the cheese is melted and bubbly.
- Garnish with fresh basil leaves, if desired.
- Serve the Keto Eggplant Parmesan hot.

🥣	**Preparation Time : 20 min**
🍳	**Cook Time : 30 min**
🕐	**Total Time: 50 min**
🍴	**Serving : 4**

NUTRITIONAL INFO (per serving)

Calories: 400

Total Fat: 28g

Protein: 22g

Total Carbohydrates: 18g

Net Carbs: 10g

ALLERGEN

Contains nuts (almond flour) and dairy (mozzarella and Parmesan cheese).

STUFFED CABBAGE ROLLS

Stuffed Cabbage Rolls are a nutritious and comforting dish, ideal for a ketogenic diet. This version features cabbage leaves filled with a savory mixture of ground meat, vegetables, and spices, all cooked in a flavorful tomato sauce. It's a wholesome and satisfying meal that brings classic flavors to your keto-friendly table.

Ingredients

- 8 large cabbage leaves
- 1 pound ground beef or pork
- 1/2 cup cauliflower rice
- 1 small onion, finely chopped
- 2 cloves garlic, minced
- 1 egg, beaten
- 1 teaspoon paprika
- Salt and pepper, to taste
- 2 cups sugar-free tomato sauce
- Optional: fresh herbs like parsley or dill for garnish

Preparation Steps

- Preheat your oven to 350°F (175°C).
- Blanch the cabbage leaves in boiling water for 2-3 minutes until they are pliable. Drain and set aside.
- In a bowl, mix together the ground meat, cauliflower rice, onion, garlic, beaten egg, paprika, salt, and pepper.
- Lay out a cabbage leaf and place a portion of the meat mixture in the center. Fold in the sides and roll up the leaf to enclose the filling. Repeat with the remaining leaves and filling.
- Place the cabbage rolls seam-side down in a baking dish.
- Pour the tomato sauce over the cabbage rolls.
- Cover the dish with foil and bake in the preheated oven for 1 hour, or until the meat is cooked through.
- Garnish with fresh herbs, if desired, before serving.

	Preparation Time : 30 min
	Cook Time : 1 hour
	Total Time: 1 hour 30 min
	Serving : 4

NUTRITIONAL INFO (per serving)

Calories: 330

Total Fat: 18g

Protein: 25g

Total Carbohydrates: 12g

Net Carbs: 8g

ALLERGEN
Contains eggs.

KETO CARBONARA

Keto Carbonara is a delightful low-carb version of the classic Italian pasta dish. In this recipe, traditional pasta is replaced with spiralized zucchini noodles (zoodles), maintaining the creamy and indulgent experience of the original dish. With a rich sauce of eggs, cheese, and crispy bacon, it's a luxurious yet keto-friendly meal that's sure to satisfy.

Ingredients

- 4 medium zucchinis, spiralized into noodles
- 8 slices of bacon, chopped
- 2 cloves garlic, minced
- 3 large eggs
- 1 cup grated Parmesan cheese
- Salt and pepper, to taste
- Optional: chopped parsley or extra Parmesan for garnish

Preparation Steps

- In a large skillet, cook the chopped bacon over medium heat until crispy. Remove the bacon from the skillet and set aside, leaving the bacon fat in the skillet.
- Add the minced garlic to the skillet and sauté for about 1 minute, until fragrant.
- Add the spiralized zucchini noodles to the skillet and toss them in the bacon fat and garlic. Cook for 2-3 minutes until the noodles are tender but still firm. Remove the skillet from heat.
- In a bowl, whisk together the eggs and grated Parmesan cheese. Season with salt and pepper.
- Quickly pour the egg and cheese mixture over the zoodles in the skillet, tossing continuously to coat the noodles and create a creamy sauce. The residual heat will cook the eggs without scrambling them.
- Add the cooked bacon to the skillet and toss everything together.
- Serve the Keto Carbonara immediately, garnished with chopped parsley or extra Parmesan if desired.

Preparation Time : 15 min

Cook Time : 15 min

Total Time: 30 min

Serving : 4

NUTRITIONAL INFO (per serving)

Calories: 400

Total Fat: 28g

Protein: 25g

Total Carbohydrates: 8g

Net Carbs: 6g

ALLERGEN
Contains eggs and dairy (Parmesan cheese)

BAKED LEMON HERB CHICKEN

Baked Lemon Herb Chicken is a flavorful and healthy keto dinner option. This dish features chicken breasts marinated in a lemon herb mixture, then baked to perfection. The result is a juicy and aromatic chicken dish that is not only easy to prepare but also packed with refreshing flavors.

Ingredients

- 4 boneless, skinless chicken breasts
- Juice and zest of 2 lemons
- 1/4 cup olive oil
- 2 cloves garlic, minced
- 1 tablespoon fresh rosemary, chopped
- 1 tablespoon fresh thyme, chopped
- Salt and pepper, to taste
- Optional: additional lemon slices and fresh herbs for garnish

Preparation Steps

- In a bowl, whisk together lemon juice and zest, olive oil, minced garlic, rosemary, thyme, salt, and pepper to create the marinade.
- Place the chicken breasts in a large resealable bag or a shallow dish. Pour the marinade over the chicken, ensuring each piece is well coated. Seal or cover and refrigerate for at least 1 hour, or overnight for more flavor.
- Preheat your oven to 375°F (190°C).
- Arrange the marinated chicken breasts in a baking dish. Pour any extra marinade over the chicken.
- Bake in the preheated oven for 25-30 minutes, or until the chicken is cooked through and reaches an internal temperature of 165°F (74°C).
- Optional: Garnish with additional lemon slices and fresh herbs.
- Serve the Baked Lemon Herb Chicken hot, accompanied by your favorite keto-friendly sides.

 Preparation Time : 10 min

 Cook Time : 30 min

Total Time: 40 min (excluding marinating time)

Serving : 4

NUTRITIONAL INFO (per serving)

Calories: 220

Total Fat: 14g

Protein: 24g

Total Carbohydrates: 2g

Net Carbs: 1g

ALLERGEN
No major allergens.

PORTOBELLO MUSHROOM PIZZAS

Portobello Mushroom Pizzas offer a unique and healthy twist on traditional pizza, perfectly aligning with a ketogenic diet. These mini pizzas use portobello mushroom caps as a base instead of dough, creating a delicious low-carb alternative. Topped with your favorite pizza ingredients, they're a savory and satisfying option for a keto-friendly meal.

Ingredients

- 4 large portobello mushroom caps, stems removed
- 1 cup sugar-free marinara or pizza sauce
- 1 cup shredded mozzarella cheese
- 1/2 cup pepperoni slices (or other keto-friendly toppings like cooked sausage, bacon, bell peppers, onions)
- 2 tablespoons olive oil
- Salt and pepper, to taste
- Optional: fresh basil or oregano for garnish

Preparation Steps

- Preheat your oven to 375°F (190°C).
- Clean the portobello mushroom caps with a damp paper towel and gently scrape out the gills with a spoon.
- Brush both sides of each mushroom cap with olive oil and season with salt and pepper.
- Place the mushroom caps on a baking sheet, gill-side up, and bake for 5 minutes to release some of their moisture.
- Remove the mushrooms from the oven and spread each cap with marinara sauce.
- Sprinkle shredded mozzarella cheese over the sauce.
- Add pepperoni slices or other keto-friendly toppings of your choice.
- Return the mushroom caps to the oven and bake for an additional 10 minutes, or until the cheese is melted and bubbly.
- Garnish with fresh basil or oregano, if desired.

	Preparation Time : 15 min
	Cook Time : 15 min
	Total Time: 30 min
	Serving : 4

NUTRITIONAL INFO (per serving)

Calories: 250

Total Fat: 18g

Protein: 15g

Total Carbohydrates: 6g

Net Carbs: 4g

ALLERGEN
Contains dairy (mozzarella cheese)

KETO CHICKEN FAJITA BOWL

Keto Chicken Fajita Bowl is a flavorful and nutritious meal that brings the essence of fajitas to a low-carb, keto-friendly format. This dish features well-seasoned chicken, sautéed peppers and onions, and a variety of toppings, all served over cauliflower rice. It's a vibrant and satisfying meal that's perfect for anyone looking to enjoy the flavors of Mexican cuisine on a ketogenic diet.

Ingredients

- For the Chicken and Vegetables:
- 2 boneless, skinless chicken breasts, sliced into strips
- 2 bell peppers (any color), sliced
- 1 large onion, sliced
- 2 tablespoons olive oil
- 1 tablespoon chili powder
- 1 teaspoon cumin
- 1 teaspoon paprika
- Salt and pepper, to taste
- For the Cauliflower Rice:
- 1 large head cauliflower, riced
- 1 tablespoon olive oil
- Salt and pepper, to taste
- Optional Toppings:
- Sliced avocado
- Shredded cheese
- Sour cream
- Fresh cilantro
- Lime wedges

Preparation Steps

- In a large skillet, heat 1 tablespoon of olive oil over medium-high heat. Add the chicken strips and season with chili powder, cumin, paprika, salt, and pepper. Cook until the chicken is browned and cooked through. Remove from the skillet and set aside.
- In the same skillet, add another tablespoon of olive oil. Sauté the sliced bell peppers and onion until they are tender and slightly caramelized.
- For the cauliflower rice, heat 1 tablespoon of olive oil in a separate skillet. Add the riced cauliflower, season with salt and pepper, and cook until tender, about 5-7 minutes.
- To assemble the bowls, divide the cauliflower rice among four bowls. Top with the cooked chicken, sautéed peppers and onions.
- Add your choice of optional toppings, such as sliced avocado, shredded cheese, sour cream, fresh cilantro, and a squeeze of lime juice.
- Serve the Keto Chicken Fajita Bowls immediately.

🥣	**Preparation Time : 15 min**
🥄	**Cook Time : 20 min**
🕐	**Total Time: 35 min**
🍴	**Serving : 4**

NUTRITIONAL INFO (per serving)

Calories: 250

Total Fat: 12g

Protein: 25g

Total Carbohydrates: 10g

Net Carbs: 6g

ALLERGEN
No major allergens in the base recipe. Optional toppings may contain dairy.

ZUCCHINI LASAGNA

Zucchini Lasagna is a fantastic keto-friendly version of the classic Italian dish. This recipe replaces traditional lasagna noodles with thinly sliced zucchini, making it low in carbs but high in flavor. Layered with a hearty meat sauce, cheese, and fresh herbs, it's a comforting and satisfying meal that's perfect for anyone looking for a healthier alternative to pasta-based lasagna.

Ingredients

- 3 large zucchinis, sliced lengthwise into thin strips
- 1 pound ground beef or Italian sausage
- 1 small onion, chopped
- 2 cloves garlic, minced
- 1 cup sugar-free marinara sauce
- 1 cup ricotta cheese
- 1 egg
- 2 cups shredded mozzarella cheese
- 1/2 cup grated Parmesan cheese
- 1 tablespoon olive oil
- Salt and pepper, to taste
- Optional: fresh basil or oregano for seasoning

Preparation Steps

- Preheat your oven to 375°F (190°C).
- Heat olive oil in a skillet over medium heat. Add the ground meat, onion, and garlic. Cook until the meat is browned. Drain excess fat.
- Stir in the marinara sauce, bring to a simmer, and cook for an additional 5 minutes. Season with salt and pepper. Set aside.
- In a bowl, mix together the ricotta cheese, egg, and a pinch of salt and pepper.
- Arrange a layer of zucchini slices to cover the bottom of a baking dish.
- Spread half of the meat sauce over the zucchini layer.
- Spread half of the ricotta mixture over the meat sauce.
- Sprinkle a layer of mozzarella and Parmesan cheese.
- Repeat the layers: zucchini, meat sauce, ricotta mixture, and cheeses.
- Cover with foil and bake for 30 minutes. Remove the foil and bake for another 15 minutes, or until the cheese is bubbly and golden.
- Let the lasagna rest for 10 minutes before slicing.
- Serve garnished with fresh basil or oregano, if desired.

Preparation Time : 20 min

Cook Time : 45 min

Total Time: 1 hour 5 min

Serving : 4

NUTRITIONAL INFO (per serving)

Calories: 450

Total Fat: 28g

Protein: 36g

Total Carbohydrates: 12g

Net Carbs: 8g

ALLERGEN
Contains dairy (ricotta, mozzarella, Parmesan cheese) and eggs.

GRILLED SALMON WITH AVOCADO SALSA

Grilled Salmon with Avocado Salsa is a delightful and healthy keto-friendly dish that combines the rich flavors of grilled salmon with the freshness of avocado salsa. This meal is not only visually appealing but also packed with healthy fats and nutrients, making it a perfect choice for a light yet satisfying dinner.

Ingredients

- 4 salmon fillets (about 6 ounces each)
- 2 tablespoons olive oil
- Salt and pepper, to taste

-For the Avocado Salsa:

- 2 ripe avocados, diced
- 1/2 red onion, finely chopped
- 1 small tomato, diced
- Juice of 1 lime
- 1/4 cup fresh cilantro, chopped
- Salt and pepper, to taste

Preparation Steps

- Preheat your grill to medium-high heat.
- Brush the salmon fillets with olive oil and season them with salt and pepper.
- Grill the salmon for about 5 minutes on each side, or until desired doneness is achieved.
- While the salmon is grilling, prepare the avocado salsa. In a bowl, combine the diced avocado, red onion, tomato, lime juice, and cilantro. Season with salt and pepper and mix gently.
- Once the salmon is cooked, remove it from the grill and let it rest for a few minutes.
- Serve the grilled salmon with a generous topping of avocado salsa.
- Optionally, garnish with additional cilantro or lime wedges.

🥣	**Preparation Time : 15 min**
🥘	**Cook Time : 10 min**
🕐	**Total Time: 25 min**
🍴	**Serving : 4**

NUTRITIONAL INFO (per serving)

Calories: 380

Total Fat: 25g

Protein: 30g

Total Carbohydrates: 10g

Net Carbs: 6g

ALLERGEN
Fish (salmon)

STUFFED PORK CHOPS

Stuffed Pork Chops are a delightful twist on a classic dish, perfect for those following a ketogenic diet. These chops are filled with a savory mixture of cheese and herbs, offering a burst of flavor in every bite. The stuffing not only adds taste but also keeps the pork chops moist and tender, making them a satisfying and elegant dinner option.

Ingredients

- 4 thick-cut pork chops
- 1/2 cup cream cheese, softened
- 1/4 cup grated Parmesan cheese
- 2 cloves garlic, minced
- 1 tablespoon fresh thyme, chopped (or 1 teaspoon dried thyme)
- Salt and pepper, to taste
- 2 tablespoons olive oil

Preparation Steps

- Preheat your oven to 375°F (190°C).
- Make a pocket in each pork chop by slicing into the side of the chop without cutting all the way through.
- In a bowl, mix together the cream cheese, Parmesan cheese, minced garlic, and thyme. Season with salt and pepper.
- Stuff each pork chop pocket with an equal amount of the cheese mixture. Secure the opening with toothpicks if necessary.
- Season the outside of the pork chops with salt and pepper.
- Heat olive oil in a skillet over medium-high heat. Sear the pork chops for 2-3 minutes on each side, until golden brown.
- Transfer the pork chops to a baking dish and bake in the preheated oven for 20 minutes, or until the pork chops are cooked through and reach an internal temperature of 145°F (63°C).
- Remove from the oven and let rest for a few minutes before serving.

🥣	**Preparation Time : 20 min**
🥄	**Cook Time : 25 min**
🕐	**Total Time: 45 min**
🍴	**Serving : 4**

NUTRITIONAL INFO (per serving)

Calories: 400

Total Fat: 28g

Protein: 35g

Total Carbohydrates: 2g

Net Carbs: 2g

ALLERGEN
Contains dairy (cream cheese, Parmesan cheese)

BAKED COD WITH PARMESAN AND PESTO

Baked Cod with Parmesan and Pesto is a light yet flavorful dish, perfect for those on a ketogenic diet. This recipe features tender cod fillets topped with a rich combination of Parmesan cheese and pesto, creating a delicious crust that enhances the natural flavors of the fish. It's a simple and elegant meal that's easy to prepare, making it ideal for a quick weeknight dinner or a special occasion.

Ingredients

- 4 cod fillets (about 6 ounces each)
- 1/2 cup grated Parmesan cheese
- 1/4 cup pesto sauce
- 2 tablespoons olive oil
- Salt and pepper, to taste
- Optional: lemon wedges and fresh herbs for garnish

Preparation Steps

- Preheat your oven to 400°F (200°C).
- Arrange the cod fillets in a greased baking dish. Season them with salt and pepper.
- In a small bowl, mix together the grated Parmesan cheese and pesto sauce.
- Spread the Parmesan-pesto mixture evenly over the top of each cod fillet.
- Drizzle olive oil over the fillets.
- Bake in the preheated oven for 12-15 minutes, or until the fish flakes easily with a fork and the topping is golden and crispy.
- Serve the Baked Cod with Parmesan and Pesto hot, garnished with lemon wedges and fresh herbs if desired.

Preparation Time : 10 min

Cook Time : 15 min

Total Time: 25 min

Serving : 4

NUTRITIONAL INFO (per serving)

Calories: 300

Total Fat: 18g

Protein: 30g

Total Carbohydrates: 2g

Net Carbs: 2g

ALLERGEN
Contains fish (cod) and dairy (Parmesan cheese)

BALSAMIC GLAZED PORK LOIN

Balsamic Glazed Pork Loin is a succulent and flavorful dish, ideal for a keto-friendly meal. The pork loin is roasted to perfection and then glazed with a rich balsamic reduction, creating a dish with a perfect balance of savory and slightly sweet flavors. This elegant and easy-to-prepare recipe is sure to become a favorite for any occasion.

Ingredients

- 1 pork loin roast (about 2 pounds)
- 2 tablespoons olive oil
- Salt and pepper, to taste
- 1/2 cup balsamic vinegar
- 2 tablespoons sugar-free sweetener (e.g., erythritol or stevia)
- 1 teaspoon garlic powder
- 1 teaspoon dried rosemary
- Optional: fresh herbs for garnish

Preparation Steps

- Preheat your oven to 350°F (175°C).
- Rub the pork loin with olive oil, salt, pepper, garlic powder, and dried rosemary.
- Place the pork loin in a roasting pan and roast in the preheated oven for about 1 hour, or until the internal temperature reaches 145°F (63°C).
- While the pork is roasting, prepare the balsamic glaze. In a small saucepan, combine the balsamic vinegar and sugar-free sweetener. Bring to a simmer over medium heat and reduce until the mixture thickens into a glaze, about 15 minutes.
- Once the pork loin is cooked, remove it from the oven and let it rest for 10 minutes.
- Slice the pork loin and drizzle the balsamic glaze over the slices.
- Garnish with fresh herbs, if desired, before serving.

 Preparation Time : 15 min

 Cook Time : 1 hour

Total Time: 1 hour 15 min

Serving : 4

NUTRITIONAL INFO (per serving)

Calories: 320

Total Fat: 14g

Protein: 40g

Total Carbohydrates: 3g

Net Carbs: 3g

ALLERGEN
No major allergens

KETO JAMBALAYA

Keto Jambalaya brings a low-carb twist to the classic Cajun dish. This flavorful recipe is packed with chicken, sausage, and shrimp, cooked with a blend of spices and vegetables, but replaces traditional rice with cauliflower rice to fit a ketogenic diet. It's a hearty, spicy, and satisfying meal that captures the essence of Southern cooking in a keto-friendly way.

Ingredients

- 1 pound chicken breasts or thighs, cut into bite-sized pieces
- 1/2 pound andouille sausage, sliced
- 1/2 pound shrimp, peeled and deveined
- 4 cups cauliflower rice
- 1 large bell pepper, diced
- 1 medium onion, diced
- 2 stalks celery, diced
- 3 cloves garlic, minced
- 1 can (14.5 ounces) diced tomatoes, with juice
- 1 cup chicken broth
- 2 tablespoons olive oil
- 1 tablespoon Cajun seasoning
- 1 teaspoon smoked paprika
- 1/2 teaspoon dried thyme
- Salt and pepper, to taste
- - Optional: sliced green onions or parsley for garnish

Preparation Steps

- Heat 1 tablespoon olive oil in a large skillet or Dutch oven over medium-high heat. Add the chicken and sausage, and cook until browned. Remove from the skillet and set aside.
- In the same skillet, add another tablespoon of olive oil. Sauté the onion, bell pepper, and celery until softened, about 5 minutes.
- Add the minced garlic and cook for an additional minute.
- Stir in the Cajun seasoning, smoked paprika, and dried thyme. Cook for 1 minute to release the flavors.
- Add the cauliflower rice to the skillet, stirring to combine with the vegetables and spices.
- Por in the diced tomatoes with juice and chicken broth. Stir and bring to a simmer.
- Return the cooked chicken and sausage to the skillet. Reduce heat to medium-low and simmer for 20 minutes.
- Add the shrimp to the skillet and cook until they are pink and cooked through, about 5 minutes.
- Season with salt and pepper to taste.
- Garnish with sliced green onions or parsley, if desired, before serving.

 Preparation Time : 20 min

Cook Time : 40 min

 Total Time: 1 hour

Serving : 4

NUTRITIONAL INFO (per serving)

Calories: 400

Total Fat: 22g

Protein: 35g

Total Carbohydrates: 12g

Net Carbs: 8g

ALLERGEN
Contains shellfish (shrimp).

CREAMY TUSCAN GARLIC CHICKEN

Creamy Tuscan Garlic Chicken is a luxurious and flavorful dish that fits beautifully into a ketogenic diet. This recipe features tender chicken breasts cooked in a creamy sauce made with garlic, sun-dried tomatoes, spinach, and heavy cream. It's a rich and satisfying meal that brings a touch of Italian elegance to your keto dining experience.

Ingredients

- 4 boneless, skinless chicken breasts
- Salt and pepper, to taste
- 2 tablespoons olive oil
- 3 cloves garlic, minced
- 1 cup heavy cream
- 1/2 cup chicken broth
- 1/2 cup grated Parmesan cheese
- 1/2 cup sun-dried tomatoes, chopped
- 2 cups fresh spinach
- Optional: fresh basil for garnish

Preparation Steps

- Season the chicken breasts with salt and pepper.
- Heat olive oil in a large skillet over medium-high heat. Add the chicken breasts and cook until golden brown on both sides and cooked through. Remove from the skillet and set aside.
- In the same skillet, add minced garlic and sauté for 1 minute until fragrant.
- Pour in the heavy cream and chicken broth. Bring to a simmer.
- Stir in the grated Parmesan cheese until it melts into the sauce.
- Add the sun-dried tomatoes and spinach to the skillet. Cook until the spinach wilts.
- Return the cooked chicken breasts to the skillet, spooning the sauce over them.
- Cook for an additional 5 minutes, ensuring the chicken is heated through and coated with the creamy sauce.
- Serve the Creamy Tuscan Garlic Chicken hot, garnished with fresh basil if desired.

	Preparation Time : 10 min
	Cook Time : 25 min
	Total Time: 35 min
	Serving : 4

NUTRITIONAL INFO (per serving)

Calories: 450

Total Fat: 30g

Protein: 35g

Total Carbohydrates: 8g

Net Carbs: 6g

ALLERGEN
Contains dairy (heavy cream, Parmesan cheese)

10
KETO
Snacks and
Dessert
RECIPES

KETO CHOCOLATE AVOCADO MOUSSE

Keto Chocolate Avocado Mousse is a smooth, rich, and creamy dessert that's perfect for satisfying your sweet cravings on a ketogenic diet. Made with ripe avocados and cocoa powder, it's a healthy and delicious way to enjoy a chocolate treat without the carbs and sugar.

Ingredients

- 2 ripe avocados, pitted and scooped
- 1/4 cup unsweetened cocoa powder
- 1/4 cup keto-friendly sweetener (e.g., erythritol or stevia)
- 1/2 cup heavy cream or coconut cream
- 1 teaspoon vanilla extract
- A pinch of salt
- Optional: whipped cream and grated dark chocolate for garnish

Preparation Steps

- In a blender or food processor, combine the scooped avocado, cocoa powder, keto-friendly sweetener, heavy cream (or coconut cream), vanilla extract, and a pinch of salt.
- Blend everything until smooth and creamy, scraping down the sides as needed to ensure all ingredients are well incorporated.
- Taste the mousse and adjust sweetness if necessary.
- Divide the mousse into four serving dishes or cups.
- For the best texture, chill the mousse in the refrigerator for at least 30 minutes before serving.
- Optional: Garnish with a dollop of whipped cream and some grated dark chocolate right before serving.

Preparation Time : 10 min

Chill Time: 30 min

Total Time: 40 min

Serving : 4

NUTRITIONAL INFO (per serving)

Calories: 250

Total Fat: 22g

Protein: 3g

Total Carbohydrates: 12g

Net Carbs: 6g

ALLERGEN
Contains avocado

KETO CHEESE CRISPS

Keto Cheese Crisps are a delightfully crunchy and savory snack, perfect for satisfying your cravings on a ketogenic diet. These crisps are incredibly easy to make, requiring just one ingredient – cheese. They are a great alternative to traditional chips, offering a low-carb snack option that's both delicious and simple to prepare.

Ingredients

- 1 cup shredded hard cheese (such as cheddar, Parmesan, or Asiago)

Preparation Steps

- Preheat your oven to 400°F (200°C).
- Line a baking sheet with parchment paper.
- Place small heaps (about a tablespoon each) of shredded cheese on the parchment paper, spaced well apart. Flatten them slightly with the back of a spoon.
- Bake in the preheated oven for 7-10 minutes, or until the edges are golden brown and crispy.
- Remove from the oven and let the cheese crisps cool on the baking sheet for a few minutes to crisp up further.
- Once cooled, gently remove them from the parchment paper using a spatula.
- Serve the Keto Cheese Crisps as a snack on their own or with your favorite keto-friendly dips.

	Preparation Time : 5 min
	Cook Time : 7-10 min
	Total Time: 12-15 min
	Serving : 4

NUTRITIONAL INFO (per serving)

Calories: 110

Total Fat: 9g

Protein: 7g

Total Carbohydrates: 1g

Net Carbs: 1g

ALLERGEN
Contains dairy (cheese)

KETO PEANUT BUTTER FAT BOMBS

Keto Peanut Butter Fat Bombs are a delicious and satisfying treat for anyone on a ketogenic diet. These bite-sized snacks are packed with healthy fats from peanut butter and coconut oil, making them an ideal choice for a quick energy boost or a sweet craving fix. They're easy to make and perfect for keeping on hand for whenever you need a keto-friendly snack.

Ingredients

- 1 cup natural peanut butter (unsweetened and unsalted)
- 1/2 cup coconut oil
- 1/4 cup keto-friendly sweetener (e.g., erythritol or stevia)
- 1 teaspoon vanilla extract
- A pinch of salt (if peanut butter is unsalted)

Preparation Steps

- In a microwave-safe bowl, combine the peanut butter and coconut oil. Microwave for 30-45 seconds, or until the coconut oil is melted. Stir well to combine.
- Add the keto-friendly sweetener, vanilla extract, and a pinch of salt (if using). Mix until all the ingredients are well incorporated.
- Line a mini muffin pan with paper liners or use a silicone mold.
- Spoon the mixture into the muffin cups or molds, filling each one about three-quarters full.
- Place the tray or mold in the freezer and freeze for at least 1 hour, or until the fat bombs are solid.
- Once set, remove the Keto Peanut Butter Fat Bombs from the mold and store them in an airtight container in the freezer or refrigerator.

Preparation Time : 10 min

Freeze Time : 1 hour

Total Time: 1 hour 10 min

Serving : 12 fat bombs

NUTRITIONAL INFO (per serving)

Calories: 150

Total Fat: 14g

Protein: 3g

Total Carbohydrates: 3g

Net Carbs: 2g

ALLERGEN
Contains peanuts (peanut butter)

KETO BERRY AND CREAM PARFAITS

Keto Berry and Cream Parfaits are a delightful and refreshing dessert, perfect for a ketogenic lifestyle. This recipe layers luscious whipped cream with fresh, low-carb berries, creating a visually appealing and delicious treat. It's an ideal dessert for those who want something sweet without the carbs, and it's also incredibly easy to prepare.

Ingredients

- 1 cup heavy whipping cream
- 1/4 cup keto-friendly sweetener (e.g., erythritol or stevia)
- 1/2 teaspoon vanilla extract
- 1 cup mixed berries (such as raspberries, blueberries, and blackberries)
- Optional: mint leaves for garnish

Preparation Steps

- In a large bowl, whip the heavy cream with a hand mixer or stand mixer until it starts to thicken.
- Add the keto-friendly sweetener and vanilla extract to the cream. Continue to whip until stiff peaks form.
- In four serving glasses or bowls, create layers by alternating spoonfuls of the whipped cream with the mixed berries.
- Repeat the layers until all ingredients are used, finishing with a layer of whipped cream on top.
- Optionally, garnish each parfait with a few berries and mint leaves.
- For best texture, chill the parfaits in the refrigerator for about 30 minutes before serving.

Preparation Time : 15 min

Chill Time : 30 min

Total Time: 45 min

Serving : 4

NUTRITIONAL INFO (per serving)

Calories: 250

Total Fat: 22g

Protein: 2g

Total Carbohydrates: 7g

Net Carbs: 5g

ALLERGEN
Contains dairy (heavy cream)

KETO CAULIFLOWER HUMMUS

Keto Cauliflower Hummus is a delicious and innovative twist on traditional hummus, perfectly suited for a ketogenic diet. This recipe uses steamed cauliflower as a base instead of chickpeas, resulting in a low-carb alternative that maintains the creamy texture and savory flavors of the classic dip.

Ingredients

- 1 large head of cauliflower, cut into florets
- 1/4 cup tahini
- 2 tablespoons olive oil
- 2 cloves garlic, minced
- Juice of 1 lemon
- 1 teaspoon ground cumin
- Salt and pepper, to taste
- Optional: paprika and extra olive oil for garnish

Preparation Steps

- Steam the cauliflower florets until very tender, about 10 minutes.
- In a food processor, combine the steamed cauliflower, tahini, olive oil, minced garlic, lemon juice, and ground cumin. Blend until smooth.
- Season the hummus with salt and pepper to taste. Blend again to incorporate.
- Transfer the hummus to a serving bowl. Optionally, drizzle with olive oil and sprinkle with paprika for garnish.
- Serve the Keto Cauliflower Hummus with keto-friendly vegetables or low-carb crackers.

	Preparation Time : 15 min
	Cook Time : 10 min
	Total Time: 25 min
	Serving : 4

NUTRITIONAL INFO (per serving)

Calories: 120

Total Fat: 10g

Protein: 3g

Total Carbohydrates: 7g

Net Carbs: 4g

ALLERGEN
Contains sesame (tahini)

KETO ALMOND FLOUR SHORTBREAD COOKIES

Keto Almond Flour Shortbread Cookies are a delightful low-carb treat that perfectly satisfies your sweet tooth while adhering to a ketogenic diet. Made with almond flour, these cookies offer a buttery, crumbly texture similar to traditional shortbread, but without the high carb content. They are simple to make and perfect for a keto-friendly snack or dessert.

Ingredients

- 2 cups almond flour
- 1/2 cup unsalted butter, softened
- 1/3 cup keto-friendly sweetener (e.g., erythritol or stevia)
- 1 teaspoon vanilla extract
- A pinch of salt

Preparation Steps

- Preheat your oven to 350°F (175°C). Line a baking sheet with parchment paper.
- In a mixing bowl, cream together the softened butter and keto-friendly sweetener until smooth.
- Add the vanilla extract and a pinch of salt to the butter mixture and mix well.
- Gradually add the almond flour to the mixture, stirring until a dough forms.
- Roll the dough into small balls and place them on the prepared baking sheet. Gently flatten each ball with the back of a fork to create a cookie shape.
- Bake in the preheated oven for 10-12 minutes, or until the edges of the cookies are slightly golden.
- Allow the cookies to cool on the baking sheet for a few minutes before transferring them to a wire rack to cool completely.

Preparation Time : 10 min

Cook Time : 12 min

Total Time: 22 min

Serving : 12 cookies

NUTRITIONAL INFO (per serving)

Calories: 160

Total Fat: 14g

Protein: 4g

Total Carbohydrates: 4g

Net Carbs: 2g

ALLERGEN
Contains nuts (almond flour) and dairy (butter)

KETO COCONUT CHOCOLATE BARS

Keto Coconut Chocolate Bars are a decadent and satisfying treat perfect for those following a ketogenic diet. These bars feature a rich coconut base topped with a layer of dark chocolate, combining the natural sweetness of coconut with the bold flavor of chocolate. They are easy to make and serve as a great snack or dessert for anyone craving something sweet and chocolatey without the carbs.

Ingredients

- For the Coconut Layer:
- 2 cups unsweetened shredded coconut
- 1/2 cup coconut oil, melted
- 1/4 cup keto-friendly sweetener (e.g., erythritol or stevia)

-For the Chocolate Layer:
- 100g dark chocolate (at least 70% cocoa, keto-friendly)
- 1 tablespoon coconut oil

Preparation Steps

- Line an 8x8 inch (20x20 cm) baking pan with parchment paper.
- In a bowl, mix together the shredded coconut, melted coconut oil, and keto-friendly sweetener until well combined.
- Press the coconut mixture evenly into the bottom of the prepared pan, creating a compact and even layer.
- In a double boiler or microwave, melt the dark chocolate with 1 tablespoon of coconut oil until smooth.
- Pour the melted chocolate over the coconut layer, spreading it evenly.
- Refrigerate the bars for at least 1 hour, or until the chocolate is set and the coconut layer is firm.
- Once set, remove from the fridge and cut into bars.
- Store the Keto Coconut Chocolate Bars in the refrigerator.

 Preparation Time : 15 min

Chill Time : 1 hour

 Total Time: 1 hour 15 min

Serving : 12 bars

NUTRITIONAL INFO (per serving)

Calories: 200

Total Fat: 18g

Protein: 2g

Total Carbohydrates: 6g

Net Carbs: 4g

ALLERGEN
Contains coconut

KETO ZUCCHINI CHIPS

Keto Zucchini Chips are a fantastic snack for those on a ketogenic diet looking for a healthy, low-carb alternative to traditional chips. These chips are made from thinly sliced zucchini, baked until crispy, and seasoned with your choice of spices. They offer a satisfying crunch and are a great way to incorporate more vegetables into your snacking routine.

Ingredients

- 2 large zucchinis
- 1 tablespoon olive oil
- Salt and pepper, to taste
- Optional seasonings: garlic powder, paprika, or Parmesan cheese

Preparation Steps

- Preheat your oven to 200°F (95°C). Line a baking sheet with parchment paper.
- Slice the zucchinis into thin, even slices, about 1/8 inch thick.
- In a bowl, toss the zucchini slices with olive oil, salt, pepper, and any additional seasonings you prefer.
- Arrange the zucchini slices in a single layer on the prepared baking sheet.
- Bake in the preheated oven for about 2 hours, or until the zucchini slices are dried out and crispy. Flip them halfway through the cooking time for even crispiness.
- Remove the chips from the oven and let them cool on the baking sheet to crisp up further.
- Serve the Keto Zucchini Chips as a snack on their own or with your favorite keto-friendly dips.

🥣	**Preparation Time : 15 min**
🥄	**Cook Time : 2 hours**
🕐	**Total Time: 2 hours 15 min**
🍴	**Serving : 4**

NUTRITIONAL INFO (per serving)

Calories: 60

Total Fat: 4g

Protein: 1g

Total Carbohydrates: 5g

Net Carbs: 3g

ALLERGEN
No major allergens

KETO AVOCADO DEVILED EGGS

Keto Avocado Deviled Eggs are a fresh and flavorful twist on classic deviled eggs, perfect for anyone on a ketogenic diet. This recipe combines the creamy richness of avocado with the classic deviled egg filling, resulting in a delightful appetizer or snack that's not only low in carbs but also packed with healthy fats.

Ingredients

- 4 large eggs
- 1 ripe avocado
- 2 tablespoons mayonnaise
- 1 teaspoon Dijon mustard
- Juice of 1/2 lemon
- Salt and pepper, to taste
- Optional: paprika or fresh herbs for garnish

Preparation Steps

- Place the eggs in a pot and cover them with water. Bring to a boil, then reduce heat and simmer for 10 minutes.
- Remove the eggs from the heat, drain the hot water, and immediately submerge them in ice water to stop the cooking process. Once cooled, peel the eggs.
- Slice the eggs in half lengthwise. Remove the yolks and place them in a bowl.
- In the bowl with the egg yolks, add the avocado, mayonnaise, Dijon mustard, and lemon juice. Mash and mix everything together until smooth. Season with salt and pepper to taste.
- Spoon or pipe the avocado mixture back into the egg whites.
- Garnish with a sprinkle of paprika or fresh herbs, if desired.
- Serve the Keto Avocado Deviled Eggs chilled.

🥣	**Preparation Time : 15 min**
🥄	**Cook Time : 10 min**
⏱	**Total Time: 25 min**
🍴	**Serving : 4 (2 halves per serving)**

NUTRITIONAL INFO (per serving)

Calories: 150

Total Fat: 12g

Protein: 6g

Total Carbohydrates: 2g

Net Carbs: 1g

ALLERGEN
Contains eggs

KETO LEMON CHEESECAKE JARS

Keto Lemon Cheesecake Jars offer a delightful and refreshing dessert option for those on a ketogenic diet. These individual servings feature a creamy lemon-flavored cheesecake filling, layered with a crumbly almond flour base, all served in convenient jars. They're perfect for satisfying your sweet tooth without the carbs and sugar of traditional cheesecake.

Ingredients

- For the Crust:
  - 1 cup almond flour
  - 2 tablespoons butter, melted
  - 1 tablespoon keto-friendly sweetener (e.g., erythritol or stevia)
- For the Cheesecake Filling:
  - 8 ounces cream cheese, softened
  - 1/4 cup keto-friendly sweetener
  - Zest and juice of 1 lemon
  - 1/2 cup heavy whipping cream
  - 1 teaspoon vanilla extract

Preparation Steps

- In a bowl, mix together the almond flour, melted butter, and sweetener to form the crust mixture. Divide the mixture evenly among 4 small jars, pressing it into the bottom of each jar to form a crust layer.
- In a separate bowl, beat the softened cream cheese with the sweetener until smooth.
- Add the lemon zest, lemon juice, and vanilla extract to the cream cheese mixture and mix well.
- In another bowl, whip the heavy whipping cream until stiff peaks form.
- Gently fold the whipped cream into the cream cheese mixture to keep it light and airy.
- Spoon or pipe the cheesecake filling into the jars on top of the crust layer.
- Refrigerate the cheesecake jars for at least 2 hours to allow them to set.
- Serve the Keto Lemon Cheesecake Jars chilled.

🥣	**Preparation Time : 20 min**
🥄	**Chill Time : 2 hours**
🕐	**Total Time: 2 hours 20 min**
🍴	**Serving : 4 jars**

NUTRITIONAL INFO (per serving)

Calories: 400

Total Fat: 36g

Protein: 8g

Total Carbohydrates: 8g

Net Carbs: 4g

ALLERGEN
Contains nuts (almond flour) and dairy (cream cheese, heavy cream, butter)

105

28 DAY
MEAL
plan

DAY 1-7 MEAL PLAN

	BREAKFAST	LUNCH	SNACK	DINNER
MON	CLASSIC KETO OMELETTE (PAG. 30) 1 GLASS OF WATER (8 OZ), 1 CUP OF BLACK COFFEE OR HERBAL TEA	KETO COBB SALAD (PAG. 52) 2 GLASSES OF WATER (16 OZ)	KETO CHOCOLATE AVOCADO MOUSSE (PAG. 96) 1 GLASS OF WATER (8 OZ)	LEMON BUTTER SALMON (PAG. 74) 2 GLASSES OF WATER (16 OZ)
TUE	GREEK YOGURT WITH NUTS AND BERRIES (PAG. 32) 1 GLASS OF WATER (8 OZ), 1 CUP OF GREEN TEA	GRILLED CHICKEN CAESAR SALAD (PAG. 53) 2 GLASSES OF WATER (16 OZ)	KETO CHEESE CRISPS (PAG. 97) 1 GLASS OF WATER (8 OZ)	KETO CHILI (PAG. 76) 2 GLASSES OF WATER (16 OZ)
WED	ALMOND FLOUR PANCAKES (PAG. 35) 1 GLASS OF WATER (8 OZ), 1 CUP OF HERBAL TEA	ZUCCHINI NOODLE ALFREDO (PAG. 54) 2 GLASSES OF WATER (16 OZ)	KETO PEANUT BUTTER FAT BOMBS (PAG. 98) 1 GLASS OF WATER (8 OZ)	BACON-WRAPPED PORK TENDERLOIN (PAG. 77) 2 GLASSES OF WATER (16 OZ)
THU	COCONUT CHIA PUDDING (PAG. 36) 1 GLASS OF WATER (8 OZ), 1 CUP OF BLACK COFFEE OR HERBAL TEA	TUNA SALAD STUFFED AVOCADOS (PAG. 55) 2 GLASSES OF WATER (16 OZ)	KETO BERRY AND CREAM PARFAITS (PAG. 99) 1 GLASS OF WATER (8 OZ)	GARLIC BUTTER STEAK BITES (PAG. 78) 2 GLASSES OF WATER (16 OZ)
FRI	KETO BREAKFAST SMOOTHIE (PAG. 37) 1 GLASS OF WATER (8 OZ), 1 CUP OF GREEN TEA	KETO BLT WRAP (PAG. 56) 2 GLASSES OF WATER (16 OZ)	KETO CAULIFLOWER HUMMUS (PAG. 100) 1 GLASS OF WATER (8 OZ)	CAULIFLOWER FRIED RICE WITH CHICKEN (PAG. 79) 2 GLASSES OF WATER (16 OZ)
SAT	KETO SPINACH AND FETA BREAKFAST MUFFINS (PAG. 38) 1 GLASS OF WATER (8 OZ), 1 CUP HERBAL TEA	BROCCOLI AND CHEESE SOUP (PAG. 57) 2 GLASSES OF WATER (16 OZ)	KETO ALMOND FLOUR SHORTBREAD COOKIES (PAG. 101) 1 GLASS OF WATER (8 OZ)	KETO SHRIMP AND BROCCOLI STIR-FRY (PAG. 80) 2 GLASSES OF WATER (16 OZ)
SUN	ZUCCHINI FRITTERS (PAG. 39) 1 GLASS OF WATER (8 OZ), 1 CUP OF BLACK COFFEE OR HERBAL TEA	KETO TURKEY AND CHEESE ROLL-UPS (PAG. 58) 2 GLASSES OF WATER (16 OZ)	KETO COCONUT CHOCOLATE BARS (PAG. 102) 1 GLASS OF WATER (8 OZ)	KETO EGGPLANT PARMESAN (PAG. 81) 2 GLASSES OF WATER (16 OZ)

DAY 8-14 MEAL PLAN

	BREAKFAST	LUNCH	SNACK	DINNER
MON	SMOKED SALMON AND CREAM CHEESE ROLL-UPS (PAG. 40) 1 GLASS OF WATER (8 OZ), 1 CUP OF BLACK COFFEE OR HERBAL TEA	STUFFED BELL PEPPERS (PAG. 59) 2 GLASSES OF WATER (16 OZ)	KETO ZUCCHINI CHIPS (PAG. 103) 1 GLASS OF WATER (8 OZ)	KETO CARBONARA (PAG. 83) 2 GLASSES OF WATER (16 OZ)
TUE	HAM AND CHEESE STUFFED MUSHROOMS (PAG. 42) 1 GLASS OF WATER (8 OZ), 1 CUP OF HERBAL TEA	EGG SALAD LETTUCE WRAPS (PAG. 60) 2 GLASSES OF WATER (16 OZ)	KETO AVOCADO DEVILED EGGS (PAG. 104) 1 GLASS OF WATER (8 OZ)	BAKED LEMON HERB CHICKEN (PAG. 84) 2 GLASSES OF WATER (16 OZ)
WED	KETO BREAKFAST 'PORRIDGE' (PAG. 43) 1 GLASS OF WATER (8 OZ), 1 CUP OF BLACK COFFEE OR GREEN TEA	CAULIFLOWER RICE STIR-FRY (PAG. 61) 2 GLASSES OF WATER (16 OZ)	KETO COCONUT CHOCOLATE BARS (PAG. 102) 1 GLASS OF WATER (8 OZ)	GRILLED SALMON WITH AVOCADO SALSA (PAG. 88) 2 GLASSES OF WATER (16 OZ)
THU	SAUSAGE AND PEPPER SKILLET (PAG. 44) 1 GLASS OF WATER (8 OZ), 1 CUP OF BLACK COFFEE OR HERBAL TEA	SHRIMP AVOCADO SALAD (PAG. 62) 2 GLASSES OF WATER (16 OZ)	KETO CHEESE CRISPS (PAG. 97) 1 GLASS OF WATER (8 OZ)	KETO CHICKEN PARMESAN (PAG. 75) 2 GLASSES OF WATER (16 OZ)
FRI	KETO VEGGIE BREAKFAST SCRAMBLE (PAG. 45) 1 GLASS OF WATER (8 OZ), 1 CUP OF GREEN TEA	KETO BEEF TACOS (PAG. 63) 2 GLASSES OF WATER (16 OZ)	KETO PEANUT BUTTER FAT BOMBS (PAG. 98) 1 GLASS OF WATER (8 OZ)	STUFFED CABBAGE ROLLS (PAG. 82) 2 GLASSES OF WATER (16 OZ)
SAT	FLAXSEED KETO WRAPS (PAG. 46) 1 GLASS OF WATER (8 OZ), 1 CUP HERBAL TEA (OPTIONAL)	CHICKEN AVOCADO CAPRESE SALAD (PAG. 64) 2 GLASSES OF WATER (16 OZ)	KETO BERRY AND CREAM PARFAITS (PAG. 99) 1 GLASS OF WATER (8 OZ)	KETO CHILI (PAG. 76) 2 GLASSES OF WATER (16 OZ)
SUN	COTTAGE CHEESE BOWL (PAG. 49) 1 GLASS OF WATER (8 OZ), 1 CUP OF GREEN TEA	SPINACH AND FETA STUFFED CHICKEN (PAG. 65) 2 GLASSES OF WATER (16 OZ)	KETO ALMOND FLOUR SHORTBREAD COOKIES (PAG. 101) 1 GLASS OF WATER (8 OZ)	PORTOBELLO MUSHROOM PIZZAS (PAG. 85) 2 GLASSES OF WATER (16 OZ)

DAY 15-21 MEAL PLAN

	BREAKFAST	LUNCH	SNACK	DINNER
MON	EGG MUFFINS WITH SPINACH AND CHEESE (PAG. 48) 1 GLASS OF WATER (8 OZ), 1 CUP OF BLACK COFFEE OR HERBAL TEA	SALMON AND ASPARAGUS FOIL PACKS (PAG. 67) 2 GLASSES OF WATER (16 OZ)	KETO LEMON CHEESECAKE JARS (PAG. 105) 1 GLASS OF WATER (8 OZ)	GARLIC BUTTER STEAK BITES (PAG. 78) 2 GLASSES OF WATER (16 OZ)
TUE	KETO VEGGIE BREAKFAST SCRAMBLE (PAG. 45) 1 GLASS OF WATER (8 OZ), 1 CUP OF BLACK COFFEE OR HERBAL TEA	KETO GREEK SALAD (PAG. 69) 2 GLASSES OF WATER (16 OZ)	KETO PEANUT BUTTER FAT BOMBS (PAG. 98) 1 GLASS OF WATER (8 OZ)	ZUCCHINI LASAGNA (PAG. 87) 2 GLASSES OF WATER (16 OZ)
WED	CINNAMON FLAVORED KETO YOGURT PARFAIT (PAG. 47) 1 GLASS OF WATER (8 OZ), 1 CUP OF GREEN TEA	KETO SHEPHERDS PIE (PAG. 71) 2 GLASSES OF WATER (16 OZ)	KETO COCONUT CHOCOLATE BARS (PAG. 102) 1 GLASS OF WATER (8 OZ)	KETO CHICKEN FAJITA BOWL (PAG. 86) 2 GLASSES OF WATER (16 OZ)
THU	FLAXSEED KETO WRAPS (PAG. 46) 1 GLASS OF WATER (8 OZ), 1 CUP OF BLACK COFFEE OR HERBAL TEA	KETO TURKEY AND CHEESE ROLL-UPS (PAG. 58) 2 GLASSES OF WATER (16 OZ)	KETO CHEESE CRISPS (PAG. 97) 1 GLASS OF WATER (8 OZ)	STUFFED PORK CHOPS (PAG. 89) 2 GLASSES OF WATER (16 OZ)
FRI	KETO CAULIFLOWER HASH BROWNS (PAG. 34) 1 GLASS OF WATER (8 OZ), 1 CUP OF BLACK COFFEE OR HERBAL TEA	KETO BLT WRAP (PAG. 56) 2 GLASSES OF WATER (16 OZ)	KETO CHOCOLATE AVOCADO MOUSSE (PAG. 96) 1 GLASS OF WATER (8 OZ)	BALSAMIC GLAZED PORK LOIN (PAG. 91) 2 GLASSES OF WATER (16 OZ)
SAT	ALMOND FLOUR PANCAKES (PAG. 35) 1 GLASS OF WATER (8 OZ), 1 CUP OF GREEN TEA	KETO GREEK SALAD (PAG. 69) 2 GLASSES OF WATER (16 OZ)	KETO ZUCCHINI CHIPS (PAG. 103) 1 GLASS OF WATER (8 OZ)	KETO JAMBALAYA (PAG. 92) 2 GLASSES OF WATER (16 OZ)
SUN	KETO BREAKFAST SMOOTHIE (PAG. 37) 1 GLASS OF WATER (8 OZ), 1 CUP OF HERBAL TEA	KETO MEATLOAF (PAG. 66) 2 GLASSES OF WATER (16 OZ)	KETO AVOCADO DEVILED EGGS (PAG. 104) 1 GLASS OF WATER (8 OZ)	CREAMY TUSCAN GARLIC CHICKEN (PAG. 93) 2 GLASSES OF WATER (16 OZ)

DAY 22-28 MEAL PLAN

	BREAKFAST	LUNCH	SNACK	DINNER
MON	CHEESY SPINACH BAKED EGG (PAG. 37) 1 GLASS OF WATER (8 OZ), 1 CUP OF BLACK COFFEE OR HERBAL TEA	KETO SHEPHERDS PIE (PAG. 71) 2 GLASSES OF WATER (16 OZ)	KETO BERRY AND CREAM PARFAITS (PAG. 99) 1 GLASS OF WATER (8 OZ)	LEMON BUTTER SALMON (PAG. 74) 2 GLASSES OF WATER (16 OZ)
TUE	AVOCADO AND EGG SALAD (PAG. 31) 1 GLASS OF WATER (8 OZ), 1 CUP OF BLACK COFFEE OR GREEN TEA	GRILLED CHICKEN CAESAR SALAD (PAG. 53) 2 GLASSES OF WATER (16 OZ)	KETO COCONUT CHOCOLATE BARS (PAG. 102) 1 GLASS OF WATER (8 OZ)	KETO CHICKEN FAJITA BOWL (PAG. 86) 2 GLASSES OF WATER (16 OZ)
WED	KETO BREAKFAST 'PORRIDGE' (PAG. 43) 1 GLASS OF WATER (8 OZ), 1 CUP OF BLACK COFFEE OR HERBAL TEA	KETO TURKEY AND CHEESE ROLL-UPS (PAG. 58) 2 GLASSES OF WATER (16 OZ)	KETO ALMOND FLOUR SHORTBREAD COOKIES (PAG. 101) 1 GLASS OF WATER (8 OZ)	BAKED COD WITH PARMESAN AND PESTO (PAG. 90) 2 GLASSES OF WATER (16 OZ)
THU	CLASSIC KETO OMELETTE (PAG. 30) 1 GLASS OF WATER (8 OZ), 1 CUP OF GREEN TEA	KETO BLT WRAP (PAG. 56) 2 GLASSES OF WATER (16 OZ)	KETO CAULIFLOWER HUMMUS (PAG. 100) 1 GLASS OF WATER (8 OZ)	KETO CARBONARA (PAG. 83) 2 GLASSES OF WATER (16 OZ)
FRI	KETO CAULIFLOWER HASH BROWNS (PAG. 34) 1 GLASS OF WATER (8 OZ), 1 CUP OF BLACK COFFEE OR HERBAL TEA	CHICKEN AVOCADO CAPRESE SALAD (PAG. 64) 2 GLASSES OF WATER (16 OZ)	KETO CHEESE CRISPS (PAG. 97) 1 GLASS OF WATER (8 OZ)	ZUCCHINI LASAGNA (PAG. 87) 2 GLASSES OF WATER (16 OZ)
SAT	GREEK YOGURT WITH NUTS AND BERRIES (PAG. 32) 1 GLASS OF WATER (8 OZ), 1 CUP OF GREEN TEA	BACON-WRAPPED ASPARAGUS (PAG. 70) 2 GLASSES OF WATER (16 OZ)	KETO PEANUT BUTTER FAT BOMBS (PAG. 98) 1 GLASS OF WATER (8 OZ)	GRILLED SALMON WITH AVOCADO SALSA (PAG. 88) 2 GLASSES OF WATER (16 OZ)
SUN	BACON AND EGG CUPS (PAG. 41) 1 GLASS OF WATER (8 OZ), 1 CUP OF HERBAL TEA	CREAMY MUSHROOM CHICKEN (PAG. 68) 2 GLASSES OF WATER (16 OZ)	KETO AVOCADO DEVILED EGGS (PAG. 104) 1 GLASS OF WATER (8 OZ)	CAULIFLOWER FRIED RICE WITH CHICKEN (PAG. 79) 2 GLASSES OF WATER (16 OZ)

CONVERSION
TABLES
and
Measurements

CONVERSION TABLES AND MEASUREMENTS

Metric (ml)	U.S. Customary
5 ml	1 teaspoon
15 ml	1 tablespoon
30 ml	1 fluid ounce
100 ml	3.4 fluid ounces
240 ml	1 cup
500 ml	2.1 cups
1 liter	4.2 cups or 34 fluid ounces

Metric (grams)	U.S. Customary (oz)
30 g	1 ounce
100 g	3.5 ounces
200 g	7 ounces
500 g	1.1 pounds
1 kg	2.2 pounds

Metric (cm)	U.S. Customary
1 cm	0.39 inches
5 cm	2 inches
10 cm	3.9 inches
30 cm	12 inches (1 foot)
100 cm	39.4 inches (1.1 yards)

Metric (Celsius °C)	U.S. Customary Fahrenheit (°F)
100°C	212°F (boiling point of water)
120°C	248°F
140°C	284°F
160°C	320°F
180°C	356°F (common baking temperature)

AFTERWORD

As we conclude Keto Diet Book for Beginners Over 60, I hope this journey has been as enlightening and empowering for you as it has been for me in putting it together. The world of ketogenic living is not just about altering what's on your plate; it's about transforming your lifestyle, embracing a new understanding of nutrition, and discovering a path to wellness that transcends conventional dieting.

Throughout this book, we've explored the fundamental principles of the ketogenic diet, tailored specifically to the needs and considerations of individuals over 60. From the detailed explanations of how and why the diet works to the meticulously crafted recipes and meal plans, every element has been designed to guide you confidently along this path.

The journey through these pages was intended to provide you with recipes and meal plans and equip you with knowledge and tools to make informed decisions about your nutrition and health. Remember, knowledge is power, especially when taking charge of your health and well-being.

As you continue on your keto journey, I encourage you to keep exploring and learning. Nutrition is a field that is continually evolving, and staying informed is key to maintaining a healthy lifestyle. Don't hesitate to revisit this book's chapters, recipes, and meal plans whenever you need a refresher or inspiration.

I want to leave you with a final thought: the keto journey is personal and unique for each individual. Embrace the changes, listen to your body, and adjust as needed. Your health journey is yours alone, and you have taken an admirable step towards a healthier, more vibrant life.

Thank you for allowing me to be a part of your keto journey. May this book be a valuable companion as you explore the exciting possibilities of a ketogenic lifestyle.

To your health and happiness,

Bianca Sealey
Author of Keto Diet Book for Beginners Over 60

THANK YOU FOR PURCHASING KETO DIET BOOK FOR BEGINNERS OVER 60 IF YOU ENJOYED THE BOOK, PLEASE LEAVE A SHORT REVIEW ON AMAZON.

YOUR FEEDBACK IS IMPORTANT TO ME BUT MORE IMPORTANTLY IT WILL HELP PEOPLE DECIDE WHETHER TO BUY THIS BOOK.

Made in United States
Orlando, FL
09 September 2024

51304525R00070